A WORLD
TOO VAST

A WORLD TOO VAST

The Four Voyages of Columbus

Alexander McKee

SOUVENIR PRESS

ISBN 0 285 62964 6

Photoset in Great Britain by
Rowland Phototypesetting Ltd,
Bury St Edmunds, Suffolk
Printed in Great Britain by
WBC Print Ltd, Bristol

Contents

List of Illustrations

MAPS

Acknowledgements

The translated contemporary narratives quoted in this book are reproduced from *The Four Voyages of Christopher Columbus* edited by J. M. Cohen (Penguin, 1969), by kind permission of Mark Cohen. The maps and sketches of ships are based on contemporary pictures, redrawn by a modern shipwright, Maurice Young.

Preface

In 1892, to celebrate the 400th anniversary of the first voyage of Columbus, 'replicas' of his three vessels of exploration, built according to nineteenth-century nautical theorists, were moved across the Atlantic. The replica *Santa Maria* was actually sailed, and she developed such a dislike of the courses steered that her voyage took three times as long as that of the real *Santa Maria*. The 'replicas' of the two caravels, *Pinta* and *Nina*, were not put to this test: they were towed across the ocean by a steam tug. This enterprising venture served to underline the fact that virtually nothing was known in the nineteenth century of the actual means by which Columbus, and many other explorers of the time, made their voyages.

For the 500th anniversary preparations were begun in the United States early in the 1980s. Firstly, to establish the first landfall made by Columbus in the New World (a question not easily resolved, since his descriptions of the islands could be matched by several possible sites). Secondly, by underwater exploration through both low- and high-tech searches, to find an authentic ship or caravel of around 1500. These caravels are today regarded as the 'space capsules' of the sixteenth century, showing how greatly attitudes towards Columbus and his achievements have changed since 1892, when virtually only the Polar regions remained unexplored; all else on earth was known—or so it was thought.

In the new age of exploration Columbus and his projects have become both topical and comprehensible. Today's areas of operation are two-fold: Outer Space (the moon and beyond to the planets) and Inner Space (the dark and difficult deep seas). In both objectives the vital importance to the explorer of a talent for publicity and fund-raising, the fight to get the support of Government or Business or Royalty, can now readily be recognised.

In past centuries Columbus has been spoken of in opposite extremes —as the Hero or as the Charlatan. Or as something in between. Or as both, equally.

What should be the twentieth-century verdict on his 500th anniversary? From a modern perspective, how does he appear?

What follows is only one view. My own.

ALEXANDER MCKEE
Hayling Island, 1989

1
Columbus—Man of Mystery

Of the new heaven and the new earth, which Our Lord made—as St John writes in *Revelations*—following the words given to Isaiah, 'He made me the messenger and he showed me where to go'—all men were incredulous. But the Lord gave to my Lady the Queen the spirit of understanding, and great courage, and He made her His dear and much beloved daughter, heiress to it all. I took possession of all these lands in her royal name. All tried to justify the ignorance in which they were sunk by speaking of difficulties and expense. The Queen, on the other hand, approved my scheme and supported it with all her power. Seven years passed in discussions and nine in the enterprise itself. Remarkable and memorable events took place in those years, which no one could have conceived beforehand.

Now I have reached a state in which even the vilest creature feels capable of insulting me, and in this state I now am. If I had stolen the Indies or the holy city of which St Peter was bishop and delivered them to the Moors, they could not treat me in Spain with greater hostility . . .

The aggrieved petitioner, being carried back to Spain in chains, was Christopher Columbus; the year, 1500. The bravest and boldest project of all time, embarked on in 1492, had borne vicious fruits. The brave new world he had discovered, riven by greed, had already become a horror.

Some parts of the story—including the character of the leading actor in the drama—are still unclear or even mysterious. No logs survive, but some parts were copied or summarised before the originals were lost. Some letters, including the extract quoted above, have been preserved into our own time. There is, however, no complete list of what has been lost.

Three centuries after Columbus was imprisoned and sent home in chains, along with some of his officers, the soldiers of another conqueror took over the castle of Simancas, where King Philip II (he who had sent the Armada to England) had collected the bulk of the Spanish archives, including much (but not all) relating to Columbus. In their new home, the soldiers of Napoleon Bonaparte lacked straw bedding for their horses (and perhaps for themselves also). But in the castle were stacked thousands of

13

legajos—bundles of documents bound with red tape. Excellent! The papers were carried away and put to real use, for the comfort of French Army horses.

What went missing we shall never know.

At least we know what Columbus looked like, although from description only (there are no contemporary portraits and later portraits that exist do not depict the same man). But those who knew him said he was a well-built man of above average height, neither fat nor thin. He had a long face with high cheekbones, an aquiline nose, light blue eyes, his complexion also light, with a ruddy tinge, and freckles. He had fair hair, with a hint of red, but his beard turned white at an early age.

He is claimed as a native-born son by seventeen Italian cities, three Spanish provinces (Andalusia, Catalonia, and Galicia), by the Armenians, the Corsicans, the French, the Greeks, the Jews—even the Swiss. He himself said that he came from Genoa, in the province of Liguria in north-western Italy. Genoa was one of the four maritime republics of Italy, the others being Amalfi, Pisa and Venice. A number of contemporary references exist, pointing to a Genoese or Ligurian background. The drawback to precise documentation is that the man changed his name several times—from Cristoforo Colombo to Cristovão Colom, to Christovam Colomo, to Collon, to Cristóbal Colón. The generally accepted view at present is that he was born in Genoa about 1451, to a family of wool weavers, his Christian name tending to rule out a wholly Jewish origin. He is said to have gone to sea at an early age, common enough practice in a great trading port like Genoa, and, despite later claims by his son that he attended the University of Pavia, people who knew him when he was grown up stated that he was a man of great intelligence but little learning.

What he certainly learned about was the sea, and in small vessels—a rough, hard, open-air, all-weather life calculated to knock the stuffing out of dilettantes, theorists and fantasists. There are hints that he sailed on trading voyages to Chios in the Aegean, to Bristol in England, and up towards Iceland, as well as in the Mediterranean, which would have given him some notion of the diversity of the seas. This was a very interesting time in which to take up a seafaring career; and he certainly went to Portugal, which was a centre of the swiftly expanding world of exploration.

At this time there was not the rigid division between captain and crew to which we are accustomed: one commands and the wage-slaves obey. Rather, the crew took a share in the ship and the trading profits of the voyage, the 'captain' (strictly speaking, the 'Master' of the ship, for 'captain' was a military term) being only the senior seaman among a crew of seamen. The set-up in a modern small fishing vessel, with all sorts of relatives and friends joining in the venture, is much more the sort of thing

Columbus would have been used to in his teens, when it seems he was acting for merchants ashore. But he would of course have absorbed the background to Mediterranean sailing—the use of the seasonal wind patterns, which had dictated the times of voyages from the days of the Phoenicians or earlier, and were well known. Not all their sailing would have been in sight of mainland coasts—and in any case, there is little reason to sneer at coastal sailors as being afraid to venture out of sight of land, because it is the coasts which are dangerous, less often the sea itself. The sudden and dramatic changes of wind direction and force—which are characteristic of the inland sea—are less deadly when there is plenty of searoom.

In Portugal, the scene was different. There were ordinary trading voyages, yes, but there were also government-sponsored probes by sea into the unknown, principally down the difficult and dangerous coasts of West Africa, aiming to round the southern tip of that continent and sail eastward to India and China and all the spices and riches of the East. For wind-driven ships, these were risky ventures. The geography was a blank, the winds and currents unknown and perhaps unfavourable, the climate deadly.

Columbus arrived in Portugal during this exciting phase of maritime expansion, but the date, even the year, is unknown. His reasons are likewise unknown. But had he remained in Genoa, his opportunities as trader, mariner and navigator must have been limited; most probably, we would never have heard of him. All we can be sure of is that in July 1478 Columbus sailed from Lisbon for the island of Madeira, a Portuguese possession out in the Atlantic to the south-west. His task was to buy sugar for the Genoese merchant Centurione. In this part of the Atlantic the prevailing current runs out to the south-west, away from Europe, as do the prevailing winds. No seaman could fail to realise this, and to compare it with the English Channel and farther north, where both prevailing current and prevailing winds trend *from* the south-west—coming in from the Atlantic towards the land. It would be most surprising if Columbus did not also acquire knowledge of the south-westward trending current and winds which prevailed not merely around Madeira but also as far south at least as the Canary Islands, then in process of being conquered by the Spaniards. And if the Portuguese, among whom he was living, did not keep too close a hold on their tongues, he would have come to know that the south-westward trending current could be traced as far south as the Cape Verde Islands.

Of course, there were old seamen's tales of land sighted out in the Atlantic, capped by cloud (in many cases that's all it was—cloud); of trunks of unknown trees washed ashore at this place or that; even of strange, shipwrecked people speaking no known tongue (some may have

15

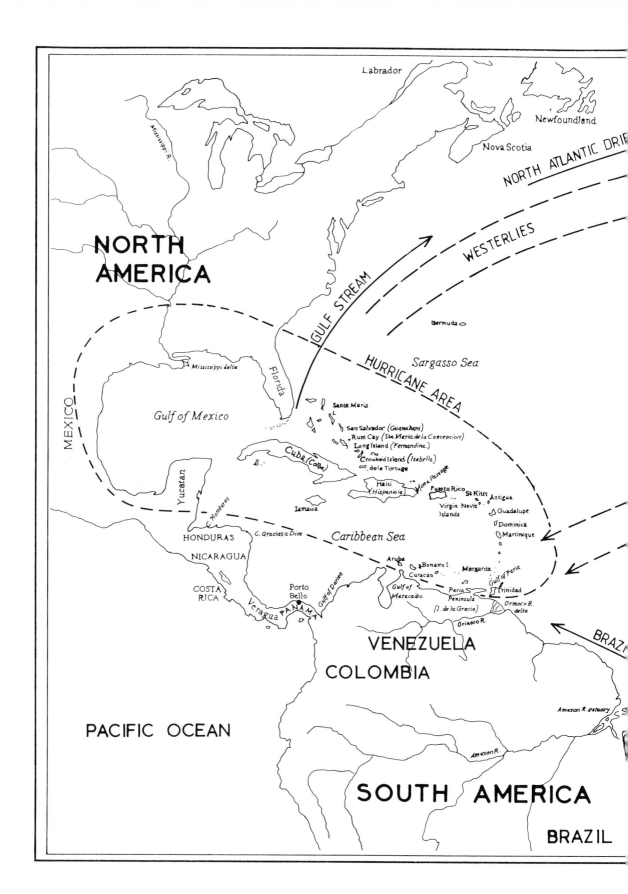

Map drawn by Maurice Young

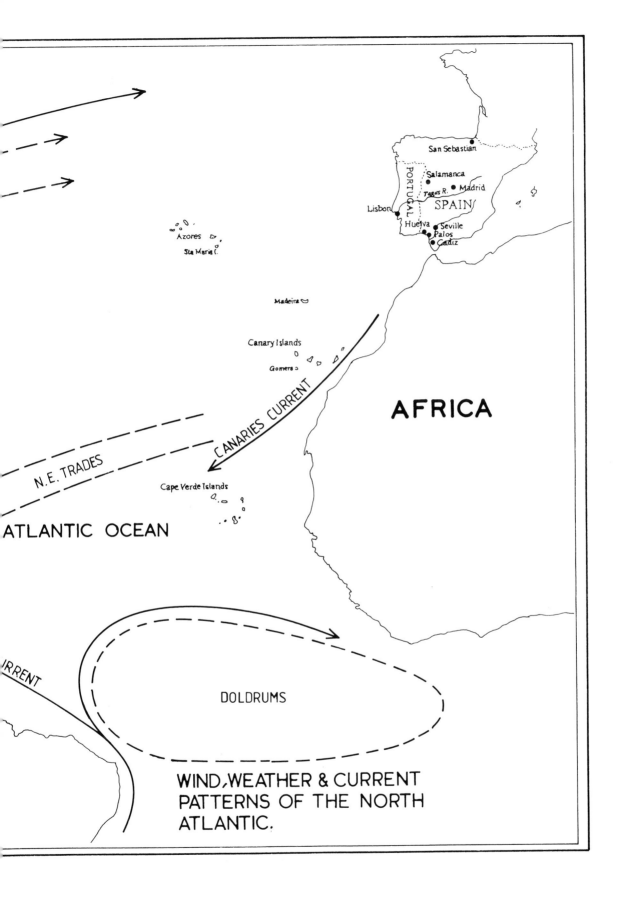

San Sebastian

Salamanca

PORTUGAL

Tagus R. ● Madrid

Lisbon SPAIN

Huelva
Seville
Palos
Cadiz

Azores

Sta Maria I.

Madeira

Canary Islands

Gomera

CANARIES CURRENT

AFRICA

N.E. TRADES

ATLANTIC OCEAN

Cape Verde Islands

RRENT

DOLDRUMS

WIND, WEATHER & CURRENT
PATTERNS OF THE NORTH
ATLANTIC.

been Eskimos). These were all clues to an enquiring mind, which would weigh them for future thought and possible action. In Africa, the Portuguese had discovered what was called the Coast of Gold, where the metal could be taken directly out of the earth. Who knew what wonders might be found out there, beyond the western horizon, by the fortunate first man to dare such a voyage?

Naturally, royal backing would be necessary, the discoveries would have to be made in the name of a Prince, otherwise they could be hijacked by any adventurer; but such backing need not be too hard to obtain or too onerous in its terms—the example of the unemployed Norman knight,

The volcanic peak of El Teide which crowns the island of Tenerife in the Canaries, surrounded as usual by a ring of cloud. Mist-shrouded peaks like this, on the islands of the Atlantic, gave rise to many tales of land to the west. *Photo: Author*

Jean de Béthencourt, in the Canaries, was fairly recent. Beginning with an expedition of his own in 1402, he had received support in men, money and honour from Henry III of Castile, occupied Lanzarote, had to fight for Fuerteventura, but was welcomed on Gomera and Hierro. Tenerife, however, was still holding out against the Spaniards when Columbus came to consider his own voyaging. The message was: If you can conquer the place for me, I'll make you King of it, giving title to you and your heirs as well as a percentage of the profits. And sometimes it was even easier: Madeira was uninhabited when discovered by the Portuguese (who were also claiming the Canaries at this time), so no bloodshed was involved.

About 1479 Columbus found a bride who came from Porto Santo, a small island near Madeira. She was Dona Felipa Moniz de Perestrello, daughter of the hereditary captain of Porto Santo. Columbus is said to have first glimpsed the lady while at Mass in Lisbon. In 1480 the couple went to Porto Santo, where their son Diego was born, and they later lived for a time in Funchal. Like the Canaries, these islands were stepping stones for exploration, southward at first and then westward, out into the Atlantic.

Dona Felipa was well born, so it might be thought that Columbus, son of a Genoese woolcarder, was coming up in the world. But both were part of the same movement at a time when there was a sense of the world opening out instead of being confined to the landlocked Mediterranean. The discovery of the Madeira archipelago had taken place around 1418–20, as a result of Portuguese ships of exploration being blown out to sea from their course southward down the west coast of Africa. The island of Porto Santo was found first. Then it was noticed that, day after day, a mass of cloud was almost always visible some 30 miles farther out into the Atlantic. The explorers ventured on and found the mountains of Madeira wrapped in cloud, in much the same way as the volcanic cone of Tenerife is often hidden from below, although baking in sunshine above. And, as at Porto Santo, they were the first men ever to look upon that scene.

It would have been impossible for Columbus, living first on Porto Santo and then by the bay of Funchal on Madeira itself, not to ponder what lay still farther out to the west.

His mother-in-law, who was related to the Braganças, the royal family of Portugal, possessed documents and marine charts which had been collected by her late husband, Dom Bartholomeu de Perestrello, the first governor of Porto Santo. She gave them to Columbus. Bartholomé Las Casas, author of *Historia de las Indias*, who knew Columbus well, wrote: 'This pleased him much, and made his desire to study cosmography the more ardent. He thought more and more of this each day, and his imagination was set aflame.'

A son of Columbus by a later love, Fernando, wrote a biography of his father which throws further light on this period. He was uncertain of the

Bartholomé Las Casas, later Bishop of the Indies, friend and biographer of Columbus and historian of the Indies.

chronology but sure of the background, and he tells us that in his mid-twenties and early thirties Columbus was living in Portugal, including the capital Lisbon, as well as in Portuguese territory overseas. that is, Madeira and Porto Santo. Part of the time he was working in Lisbon as a chart-maker with one of his younger brothers, Bartolomeo.

He obtained information about other journeys and the voyages that the Portuguese were making to Mina [the Gold Coast] and down the coast of Guinea [West Africa] at that time, and he found great satisfaction in conversing with the men who sailed in those regions. To tell the truth, I do not know if it was during the marriage [his wife Felipa died about 1483] that the Admiral sailed to Mina and Guinea, but it seems reasonable to assume that he did so. Be that as it may, one thing led to another and gave life to many thoughts, so that the Admiral, while in Portugal, began to think that, if the Portuguese could sail so far to the south, it should be possible to sail equally far to the west, and that it was logical to expect to find land in that direction. To obtain confirmation on this point, he returned to those writers on geography with whose work he was already familiar, and began to consider the astronomical arguments that might support his design, at the same time noting down all pieces of information given him by mariners and others.

Columbus may not have known how old this idea was, but Aristotle had already written in his *Treatise on Heaven and Earth*: 'The region of the columns of Hercules (Gibraltar) and that of India are bathed by the same ocean.'

It only remained to prove it.

2
How Big Is the World?

Everyone who knew anything knew that the world was round. Disregarding some aberrations of the medieval Church, the fact had been known for a long time. That the earth was a sphere had been proclaimed by Pythagoras (550 BC), Plato (400 BC), Aristotle (350 BC), and Eudoxus (also 350 BC). The moon is a sphere, the sun is a sphere; it was not very far-fetched to assume that our world also was round. To a seaman it was obvious. You had only to watch how a ship came up over the horizon as it approached—the topsails appearing first, the hull last; and in the reverse order when it was going away. An approaching ship actually climbed up the horizon.

Nowadays, from a jet aircraft at around 40,000 feet and in limitless visibility, there is proof positive. You can see the actual curve of the earth—or the ocean—bringing the thought that our world is really not all that large. But what is its actual size? This was the crucial debate among geographers and navigators for thousands of years.

To impose order on chaos geographers had agreed certain quite arbitrary assumptions, which are still made in modern times. One direction was said to be north; its opposite was called south. So a certain star was called the North Star; if it could be seen at night, you knew which way you were going. In modern times it is difficult or impossible to pinpoint, like the rest of the night sky, because of the glare from towns, cities and motorways; but in ancient times you could steer by it. Not that they were free of industrial haze, but it was very localised; not on our scale. Then again you could tell which was south (in the northern hemisphere, if the sky was clear) because that's where the sun was at its highest point. And that introduces another concept—the equator.

The geographers agreed to draw a line round the globe at its widest point. They didn't actually draw it—you won't find such a line painted on soil and sea as might a traffic warden—they just agreed to assume it was there and mark their globes accordingly. Now things were falling into place.

They made a further orderly assumption: that this fat line circling the globe at the greatest girth was cut by 360 other lines going both north and south and coming together so that they met at the North Pole and at the

South Pole. No one had ever been to either pole, but this did not matter because the lines were imaginary. These lines are not parallel (although they may seem so on a map or chart) and it was decided to call them degrees. It was as if an orange had been sliced into 360 equal segments. To calculate the circumference of the globe, all you had to know was the distance between one degree and another at the equator.

In the third century BC, a Greek astronomer called Eratosthenes estimated the circumference as 250,000 *stadia* (or 27,750 modern miles). In the second century AD another Greek, Ptolemy, a mathematician, astronomer and geographer, stated in his work *Geographike Hyohegesis* that one degree equalled 50 nautical miles; while a Moslem, Al-Farghani, living in the ninth century AD, believed the world to be larger, at 66 miles to a degree. Columbus, consulting various authorities and indulging in some speculation of his own, went about saying that the word was really quite small, one degree equalling only 45 miles. By believing, or affecting to believe, that the Moslem Al-Farghani was thinking of the short Roman mile rather than the longer Arab mile, Columbus managed to include him as a supporting authority.

In his calculations, and in the proofs of them, Columbus continues to arouse intense speculation. Just how sincerely did he believe in his own story? That he believed a great deal is certain, because of the sheer determination he exhibited year after year, in the face of discouragement and disparagement; but at some point, exactly when is unclear, he becomes a salesman, writing a marvellously optimistic prospectus. Certainly he was courtwise and knew the business fraternity. With them, it was no good being studiously careful and objective. The grand flourish and the great promise were the thing. Naturally, they would subtract substantial amounts from his claims; that was why it was necessary to make them in the first place.

Scholarly dispute about theories was one thing, but for a man who intended to put his beliefs to the proof, there was the chilling factor of range. Explorers' ships had to be small, with a shallow draft, and handy; otherwise, shipwreck on unknown reefs or banks, or embayment in some uncharted gulf, was virtually certain. That ruled out the large, capacious cargo carriers, capable of extended voyages. But the lighter, handier vessels could store only limited supplies of food and water. If the world was simply too large, and there were no islands from which water and victuals could be had, then the explorers would never return. They would perish of thirst certainly, and perhaps of hunger also, with no one to tell their tale. There were precedents—men like the Vivaldi of Genoa, who had sailed over the horizon and never come back.

Who knew what might lie out there? Human foes—perhaps? Monsters —maybe? In any event, the knife-edge of limited supplies held in a small

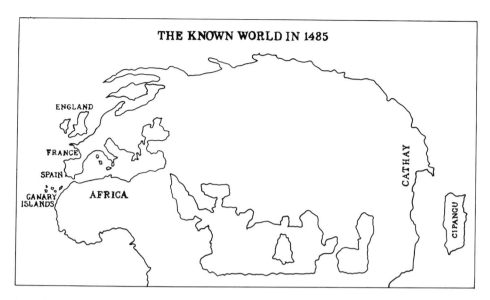

Map drawn by Maurice Young

vessel totally dependent on the vagaries of the winds in oceans unknown.

So, how big was the world?

Maps exercise their fascination over those who use them often—soldiers, for example, especially generals; but they are concerned with more than distances: they need to know the contours of the land, its rivers, its roads and (in modern times) its railways and airfields.

Charts hold an equal fascination (in modern times) for the diver who is an explorer, just as Columbus meant to be, although his horizon was the world. Localised though his field may be, the underwater explorer, before ever he goes underwater (if he is wise) studies charts, absorbs them, tries to make them yield information unguessed at by their makers. Those contours—what is their significance? Do they mark the scour of the tides around a long-lost wreck which has now disappeared into the seabed? Or this place, marked *Obstruction*; that must BE something. A wrecked ship, a crashed aeroplane, a sunken channel buoy? Who knows? No one, until you go and find out. And if you find anything important, you don't talk openly, you guard your tongue.

As chart-makers, Columbus and his brother would have kept their ears open and their mouths shut. Seamen back from exploration ventures into unknown and dangerous waters would soon be boiling over with their own exploits, even if they had been warned to keep silent (as they would be, most strictly, if in the pay of a prince). A slight show of disbelief might be enough to loose the flood, especially if the sceptic was a rival seaman.

Such were the ingredients of chart-making on the ground floor. But for a great venture, such as Columbus was pondering, globes rather than charts were appropriate; and academics rather than practical mariners. But Columbus was on optimist and looked for optimistic facts and theories. It could hardly be otherwise. Pessimists are unlikely to take up exploration and if they did, would be unlikely to succeed.

Two relevant books owned by Columbus survive, with his own marginal notes and some by his brother Bartolomeo. From these, his aim is clear. In his copy of the book by Marco Polo about his travels to the land of the Great Khan, the key words are underlined: *Pearls, precious stones, brocades, ivory, or pepper, nuts, nutmeg, cloves and an abundance of other spices.* His ambition was not to discover a new land, but to reach an immensely rich known civilisation by a new and more workable route.

So he searched for evidence that the route was both safe and short. That this was so could be proved by reading his copy, also with marginal notes, of *Imago Mundi* by Cardinal Pierre d'Ailly. Written in 1410, it was first printed about 1480. Columbus repeated in the margins what seemed to be the key points made by the French Cardinal, based on the findings of others, such as Aristotle: *Sea and land combine to form a round body . . . Between the end of Spain and the beginning of India lies a narrow sea that can be sailed in a few days . . . Six parts of the earth are habitable, and the seventh is covered with water.* And again, as with Marco Polo's book, the treasures are underlined or repeated: *The crystals and precious stones to be found in Germany, the river that carries gold dust; elephants and precious stones; aromatic spices, mountains of gold . . .* Across the ocean, the grass was most certainly greener. Little of this was actually untrue; potentially, it was all there. All that had to be discovered was the way.

Long study of Marco Polo's stories yielded a rough guide. He had lived much of his life in the East, travelled more widely both by land and by sea than anyone then or since. He gave names, places, distances, days or even months of travel. For instance, from the Court of the Great Khan, he had sailed south to Java with a fleet of fourteen ships, all of them four-masters like the greatest of European vessels, the largest having crews of 250 or more seamen. The ships carried provisions for two years and the passage to Java took eighteen months. Travelling farther south to Lesser Java, Marco noted that from this island the Pole Star could never be seen.

Java, therefore, must be south of the equator—the imaginary line around the largest girth of earth—and the lands of the Great Khan lay some 1,500 to 2,000 miles north of that. So the voyage west to Cathay and Cipangu must lie along a much lesser distance than if it had been on the equator.

But how 'high' above the equator was Cathay (Northern China)? Columbus reckoned probably due west of the Cape Verde islands; even if this was only approximately true, one could hardly miss a continent. If one strayed too far north, the landfall would be on the coast of Cipangu (Japan) or its outlying islands; if one was driven too far south, then the landfall might be in Java, still a place rich in spices. Treasure of all kinds lay to the west, there was no doubt of it. Marco Polo had spent 26 years travelling through most of the lands in the East, even India, and spoke some of the languages. He was from Venice, the worthy Italian rival of Genoa, and so in essence his tales were believable. Where he had not visited personally but relied on other people's reports, he said so. He had acquired the nickname *Il Milione*, because he was a man who talked in millions; but Columbus judged that Marco Polo spoke the truth so far as he knew it.

Now Columbus had to convince princes that Marco Polo was no liar and that he, Columbus, could reach those riches by the westward route.

As ships of exploration must be small and could not carry food, water and wine for long voyages such as the Chinese made, the way across must be shown as short and easy. So he had to become a world geographer, reaching beyond the expertise of a Lisbon chart-maker, and have that knowledge tested by scholars, some of them sceptical from the start of the views of unlearned men like Columbus.

3
The Years of Pleading

When his first wife Felipa died Columbus did not marry again, but he did take a mistress. The first-born of this liaison was Fernando Colón, who was 17 years old when his father died in 1506 and was the writer of the biography from which we have already quoted. In the eyes of the son, the father was a grand person. His biography, published in Italian in 1541, is the source for statements that Columbus was high-born and well educated, attended university and so on, in contradiction of the man's contemporaries who wrote that he was of plebeian origin, was early apprenticed to the sea, was of great natural intelligence and became a skilled navigator. Columbus, who had become a great man by his own efforts and mixed with rulers and princes as of right, did not acknowledge Fernando's mother and in turn Fernando did not admit that he was the illegitimate son of a mistress. Not, at any rate, in print for all the world to read.

Instead, there were the claims for illustrious birth and stirring tales of his father's warlike exploits, both courageous and cunning, during his early years at sea: when taken captive, tampering with the ship's compass (unnoticed by the crew); or escaping from a lost sea battle by a long swim to shore. It may be so, but perhaps, writing many years afterwards, Fernando did not recall his father's stories with complete fidelity. Or perhaps the father embroidered. Certainly, Fernando fails to tell us many things we would like to know, so that Columbus remains still a partially unknown quantity.

How, for example, did he make his first bid for royal support? All Fernando says is that his father approached King John II of Portugal (where he was then living), and that the king was not greatly interested in a project to sail out into the Atlantic in search of the Indies because his southern expeditions down the coast of West Africa to Guinea had cost much in time and money and showed no returns. No doubt that was true, so far as it went. But João Barros, a Portuguese chronicler, adds significant detail.

He came to the conclusion that it was possible to sail across the western Ocean to the island of Cipangu and other unknown lands.

For since the time of Prince Henry, when the Azores were discovered, it was held that there must be islands and other lands to the west, for nature could not have set things on earth so out of proportion that there should be more water than land, which was intended for life and the creation of souls. With these fantastic ideas which he had obtained on his continual voyages, and from talks with men who were versed in such matters and in this kingdom had great knowledge of past discoveries, he came to King John II, asking him for ships that he might sail away and discover the island of Cipangu in the western Ocean . . . When the King found that this Cristovão Colom was very proud and boastful in presenting his talents, and more fanciful and full of imagination than accurate when speaking of this island of Cipangu, he had little faith in him.

Since, however, Columbus was insistent, the King set up a commission of experts. The men asked to give their verdict on the Genoese seaman's ideas included a scientist who was also a cleric, the Bishop of Ceuta, Dom Diogo Ortiz; an astronomer who was also the king's physician, Master Rodrigo; and a famous cosmographer and astronomer, José Vicinho. They reported: There might or might not be an island such as Cipangu off the coast of Cathay; but if there was, it was too far away for a sea journey to be practical. They agreed that the Moslem Al-Farghani was right in his calculations of the size of the earth, but as a Moslem, naturally his distances were expressed in the longer Arabian miles and not the shorter Roman ones, as Columbus was arguing. The suggested voyage was not practical, the distance was far too great.

When the king refused to supply Columbus with ships for this enterprise, he did so having taken the advice of some of the most learned men of the age.

That did not deter the Genoese mariner. In 1484 he and his young son Diego left Portugal for Spain. They were bound for the court of Castile. Apart from his ambitions, Columbus had an additional reason for leaving Portugal at this time: he was being pursued by creditors.

*   *   *

In AD 711 the Arabs had begun their invasion of the Iberian peninsula by landing at Gibraltar, their advance being stemmed only in 732 when they were defeated actually inside the frontier of France. Their rule lasted many centuries, and served to spread Arab scholarship and translations of the old Greek philosophers throughout Europe. The Moors, as these Moslems were commonly called, were only gradually driven back. Internal rivalries among Spaniards helped delay the long reconquest. A step towards unity was the marriage in 1469 of two young rulers, Ferdinand of Aragon, aged 18, and Isabella of Castile, aged 19. Ten years later, in 1479, the civil strife came to an end. In 1481 a united Spain turned on the last Moorish stronghold in Europe, Granada, ruled by an equally young monarch, Muhammad Abu-Abdullah, whom the Spaniards called Boabdil. He surrendered in the spring of 1492, and Spain was free to overrun her borders and conquer other races. Columbus was present at the Spanish court when Granada fell. Now for him the time and the place were absolutely right.

For the 1480s the chronology is obscure. In 1484, on his journey to Castile, Columbus left his young son Diego, then about three years old, with his wife's married sister in Huelva; presumably because a man who

The walls of Granada, the Moorish fortress which fell to Ferdinand and Isabella in January 1492. *Courtesy Spanish National Tourist Office*

29

was planning to plead his case at court literally could not afford such a distraction, particularly if he were poor.

But first he stayed for a year or two with the Count of Medina Celi. During this period he was exploring a number of possibilities. He persuaded his brother Bartolomeo to go to England and try to get backing for the venture from the new Tudor King, Henry VII. He himself proposed to tackle the King of France about the matter. When Medina Celi learned this (as he told the Grand Cardinal of Spain in a letter), he was tempted to finance the voyage himself from his own harbour, where he had three or four caravels, a number ample for the plan the Genoese put forward. Just a few small ships of exploration, that was all it might take to discover a new route to the Indies. Then it occurred to the Count that this could be an important matter of State, and not for a mere individual. So he wrote to Isabella of Castile, and she replied that he should send Columbus to her.

According to Columbus himself, he reached the court at Cordova on 20 January, 1486. Ferdinand and Isabella were away that winter and would not return until the spring. Meanwhile Columbus had to earn his living. Probably this was the time when, as stated by the chronicler Bernáldes, Columbus was an itinerant seller of printed books in Andalusia.

And perhaps this was also the time when Columbus met Beatriz Enriques de Harana, a commoner not to be presented at court, who was besides, like the explorer himself, poor. In the autumn of 1488 she gave birth to Fernando, Columbus's second (but this time illegitimate) son. In his will, he was to ask his elder son, Diego, to provide for his mistress,

> so that she may be able to live honourably, for she is someone to whom I owe a great deal. And this shall be done so that I may satisfy my conscience, for the matter weighs heavily on my soul. This is not the place to give the reasons.

And that is about all we know of the lady. Little more in fact than we know of his wife, Felipa Moniz de Perestrello, who bore Diego and then died a few years later, in about 1483.

In December 1488 the latest small fleet of exploration, which had been sent out under Bartholomeu Dias by King John II of Portugal, sailed back into Lisbon. Two small caravels and a storeship had set out and the caravels, venturing well ahead, had been blown right round the southern point of Africa without even seeing it. Returning, this time in sight of the coast, Dias called the last southern promontory of Africa *Cabo Tormentoso*, Cape of Storms, but the Portuguese king refused to accept the discoverer's name for that fearsome dark headland. Its discovery meant that there was indeed a practical way east round Africa to the Indies, and the king renamed it Cape of Good Hope.

Only nine months earlier, King John had had second thoughts about his dismissal (on expert advice) of Columbus, and urged him to come back to Portugal, assuring the Genoese explorer that he would not be arrested, detained, accused, charged or prosecuted in any suit, civil or criminal, of any kind whatsoever. Now there no longer seemed any need to retain the western option; the eastern route round the cape was open, and in 1497–99 Vasco da Gama was to complete a voyage to India.

One of those who had watched Dias sail back in triumph to Lisbon was Columbus's brother Bartolomeo, whose mission to persuade the King of England to back the Atlantic plan had met with rejection. Some encouragement he must have had from the Spanish court, most probably from Isabella. One document summoning him to court has survived (there may have been others now lost). That was in 1489 when the monarchs were with their army besieging the Moorish forces in Baza. A year later a Royal Commission met to consider the Genoese mariner's proposal. The president was Hernando de Talavera, one of Queen Isabella's confessors; we know the name of one other member of the court, and of no one else. The Columbus project was turned down, for reasons unknown.

However, Fernando Colón, after stating that there were few geographers available then (a hint that his father's calculations had once more failed to gain acceptance by scholars) wrote that Columbus did not wish to reveal all the details of his plan, for fear that it might be stolen from him in Castile as it had been in Portugal. The reference to Portugal is obscure, but most certainly Columbus during these years was in this considerable difficulty, that if he convincingly explained just how he intended to set about the voyage—for instance, what winds and currents he intended to use—then anyone else with greater backing could perform the feat. There was no copyright in ideas, and Columbus had very clear ideas, as his actual voyages make plain.

Fernando may have been biased against the Spanish Royal Commission. He says they argued that these regions had remained unknown for thousands of years, and was it likely that this particular mariner knew more than any man who had ever lived? Others based their opposition on geography, asserting that the world was a very large place and that it would take more than three years for Columbus to reach the farthest extreme of India. Yet others maintained that the ocean was infinite and impossible to sail across. And in any case, what proof was there that habitable lands existed on the far side? And others still, or so Fernando says, put forward the commonsense argument of the literal man: Since the earth was round, a seaman who sailed away could never sail back, as he would be sailing up hill.

But Columbus was a convincing propagandist, even if for security's sake he had to halter his arguments; he conveyed a certainty and sense of

King Ferdinand of Aragon. *Courtesy of the Trustees of the British Museum*

destiny which impressed many who did not altogether follow the geographical disputations. Ferdinand and Isabella gave him hope that they might consider his proposals favourably once the Moorish question had been solved. They were determined upon the capitulation of Granada.

Isabella had been thirty-five when Columbus had his first audience with her; she was the same age as himself. As the ruler of Castile, sea matters lay in her province and she carried the bulk of the discussions. Isabella had a fair complexion with honey-coloured hair, clear eyes, a rather full face and a strong, rounded body. She was devout to a fault, sure that Spain must be cleansed of unbelievers or even half-believers. She established the Inquisition to search out Jews and Moors who had only superficially adopted the Christian faith. The best argument Columbus could use with her was to point out that the discovery of new lands would mean also that Christians would make contact with many more souls capable of salvation.

But by 1491 both the Queen and her explorer were moving into their forties. Time was passing for both of them, but more for Columbus than for the Queen. The weakness of age is no bar to statecraft, may even enhance it, but for the seaman and explorer sheer physical force and energy is a necessity. In that year, Columbus set out for France. Spain was keeping him in reserve, England had turned him down; perhaps the French court would be more far-sighted.

Taking his son Diego, now a boy of about ten, Columbus journeyed first to stay at the monastery of La Rabida near the Atlantic towns of Palos and Huelva. The Prior, Juan Pérez, played a key role in what followed, writing a letter to the Queen commending Columbus. Possibly he also introduced Columbus to the Pinzón brothers of Palos. Martin Alonso Pinzón was a notable seaman and ship-owner, reputedly the finest navigator in Andalusia. The letter to Isabella brought an instant reply. The Queen wished to see him; he should present himself at court immediately. A sum of money, 20,000 *maravedis*, was sent to Columbus via the Mayor of Palos, so that Columbus could buy himself a horse and a decent set of clothes. A man without a horse then was like a man without a car now.

So Columbus rode off to court, at that time established at the tented town of Santa Fé, once an obscure village but now Army headquarters for the Granada campaign. The encampment was being fortified and on the verge of becoming permanent. Death had travelled the roads Columbus

Queen Isabella of Castile. *Courtesy of the Trustees of the British Museum*

33

took, and ruins showed the way the war had passed; the enemy-held
battlements of the Alhambra overlooked the court of the two monarchs,
and behind the Moorish fortress city reared the mountainous backdrop of
the Sierra Nevada. There was skirmishing up front, but there was to be no
assault. The campaign was directed to achieving a capitulation on terms.
The last great stronghold of the Moors in Spain—in Europe—was to
submit without bloodshed. At the end of November 1491 the surrender
terms were signed; on 2 January, 1492 the march-in took place and the
standards of Castile and Aragon were raised on the towers of the
Alhambra.

Now, or it may have been a little before, the Columbus project was
reconsidered; and in a new light. There was a Columbus lobby: two friars,
Pérez and Deza, to argue perhaps for a harvest of new souls to be won for
Christ (and Pérez may have been the Queen's confessor); two court
counsellors, Quintanilla and Cabrera, to plead the political importance to
Spain of finding an alternative route to the one already discovered round
Africa by the Portuguese; two businessmen, Santangel and Pinello, who
could urge the commercial value of cutting out the Arab middlemen from
the luxury trade with the East. And, apart from Isabella herself, there were
two women—one a close friend, Beatriz de Bobadilla, Governor of
Gomera, one of the Canary Islands, a Spanish outpost far out into the
Atlantic just above the equator; and the Marquise de Moya who is said to
have had a relationship of a private nature with the Genoese explorer.

The decision now went in favour of Columbus. The wild scheme had
become a bandwagon and it was ready to roll. Sensing this, perhaps, when
the question of reward was raised, Columbus staked a maximum claim,
economically and in honours. His financial demand was that he should
receive one tenth of the value of the gold, silver and spices discovered,
plus one eighth of the profits of the venture. The Spanish Crown was later
to impose a 'Royal fifth' tax on the discoveries Columbus made, but for the
man himself to claim a tenth when he could not even afford to keep a
horse, must have seemed presumptuous. Even more presumptuous,
particularly to the high-born, must have appeared this foreigner's demand
for a title—he was to be made Don Cristóbal Colón, if you please! He was
to rank as an Admiral of the Ocean as well as Crown Viceroy and Governor
of any territories he might conquer.

The Service rank, although a high one, was probably not the sticking
point. There were precedents, some as recent as October 1491, when the
Galician knight Alonzo de Lugo, who had served at the siege of Granada,
put forward a plan to conquer from the local natives two islands in the
Canaries group, La Palma and Tenerife. He was given the rank of Captain
General of the Canaries, and by May 1492 had taken La Palma. Tenerife
was to prove more difficult.

The world of the Court, of nobility and command, was very small and select. Alonzo de Lugo was later to marry the beautiful heiress of Gomera, Beatriz de Bobadilla, who had been widowed in 1488 when her husband, the Governor of Gomera, Hernan Peraza, had taken a native princess, Iballa, as his mistress; the girls' relatives had fatally objected, and after killing the adulterer had besieged Beatriz and her babies in a small fort, the Torre del Conde. Rescued, and now at Court, she was the object of a mild flirtation on the part of Queen Isabella's husband, Ferdinand. No doubt he admired a woman who was as brave as she was beautiful. The island which Beatriz ruled was to be Columbus's planned last port of call before the Indies, the island where he could top up his supplies before the desperate hazard of the long voyage out into the unknown.

Probably it was the pride of the military caste, making them jib at the demand of a common-born Genoese seaman, son of a wool weaver, to be ennobled (and his offspring after him), that made them reject all the explorer's demands. They said NO! with finality. And Columbus mounted his horse, bought with the Queen's money, and rode away, having lost everything.

Then the pro-Columbus lobby got to work. Fernando Colón was to name Luis de Santangel as the man who went to the Queen and put forward a stream of reasonable arguments. Santangel was a businessman, a convert from Judaism, peculiarly at peril now. The Holy Inquisition had secured the Crown's agreement to their solution to the Jewish 'problem' —a mass expulsion of all who would not give up their religion, with death as the penalty for unauthorised return. Some of Santangel's relatives were to be burned at the stake. Nevertheless, he was able to show convincingly that it was in the best interests of Spain to back Columbus. If he failed, the cost would be small; if he succeeded, he would have more than earned everything he had asked for. And the terms of the agreement could be made to be dependent upon success, particularly the financial provisions. Columbus was sincere, he argued, being prepared to pay part of the cost himself (with money which Santangel would loan). Isabella's enthusiasm was easily rekindled; she said she was ready to pledge her jewellery to back the project, but Santangel said that would not be necessary, he would see to it.

A court functionary was sent off on a fast horse to bring Columbus back. He had only got as far as the bridge of Pinos on the road to Cordova, when he was overtaken. On 17 April, 1492, his contract was signed by both sovereigns, Ferdinand signing under the words *Yo el Rey* ('I the King') and Isabella under *Yo la Reyna* ('I the Queen').

And so the momentous voyage was launched.

4
Crewing the Caravels

The detailed orders signed by the King and Queen and countersigned by the State Secretary of Aragon, Juan de Cóloma, whose mother was Jewish, reveal much financial acumen and a dismal psychology echoing similar trains of thought in modern times.

On 30 March, 1492, de Cóloma, a *converso*, had countersigned the order for the deportation of the Jews. The action had been asked for by the Holy Office (generally known as the 'Spanish Inquisition' because the Spanish variety was so much harsher than that of any other nation). The result had been an exodus of Jews to all the major ports, such as Seville and Cadiz; so much so that the Columbus expedition could not be outfitted at these places. At Cadiz alone, the quays were crowded with some 8,000 families seeking passage either to the ports of North Africa (the Moslems were less fierce than the Christians) or to northern Italy (where the wishes of the Grand Inquisitor of Spain, Torquemada, were regarded as over-severe by the Papal authorities). The Vatican had to deal only with heretical Christian sects; in newly-united Spain and conquered Granada a substantial part of the population were not Spanish, or were unreliable *conversos*, unwilling converts to Christianity. So the refugees blocked the quaysides of the big ports in southern Spain.

On 17 April, while these distressing scenes were taking place, the contract with Columbus was signed—henceforward he was Don Cristopher—and on 30 April a mass of bureaucratic documents, including Columbus's 'passport' and letters of credit to the foreign rulers he expected to contact; but all left vague, deliberately. All countersigned, as usual, by Juan de Cóloma of Aragon.

On 23 May, 1492, a further order signed by Ferdinand of Aragon and Isabella of Castile was read aloud in the Church of St George in the port of Palos, the small haven on a bend of the Rio Tinto. Columbus had handed the document to the Mayor of Palos, who had in turn given it to the notary to read out to the people from the iron pulpit. One door of the little building looked up to the mountains of Spain. The other was called *la puerta de l'embarcadero*. Palos had been chosen as the port which would launch the expedition.

Columbus knew it well, had spent much time during the bitter waiting years discussing the project with the clergy and visiting seamen at the nearby monastery of La Rabida. But that was not the reason why the Crown had chosen Palos.

There was a financial twist. The authorities had discovered an unresolved case in their files: certain ships of Palos had imported foreign goods without Royal Permission. They decided that the sentence for smuggling, in this case, would be the provision of two caravels, equipped and stored for a year's voyage, to the Columbus expedition, 'at your burden and cost'. Columbus had been promised three vessels, but the Crown would have to pay only for the third ship; the other two were to be the unwilling gift of Palos. The news can hardly have been well received in the port, where in any event not everyone believed in the practicality of the Genoese mariner's plans.

A further shock was still to come—not merely a financial trick, but an outright insult to that little town of seafarers, and an offence to the friars of La Rabida, who conceived the project as a holy mission sent out to save souls for the church. Juan Pérez, prior of La Rabida, who had spoken for Columbus at the Court and travelled to Palos with him on this occasion, was present.

It was announced in church that all civil and penal proceedings against anyone who volunteered to serve aboard these ships would be suspended. Less politely, the criminals from the jail were being encouraged to join the expeditions.

Four men, all under sentence of death, were released from prison on condition that they went with Columbus. One was Bartolomé de Torres, who had killed a man in a fight, unintentionally; the others, the three friends who had subsequently tried to help him escape. Whoever made this choice was a wise man, for they made good, reliable seamen; and two volunteered to serve again with Columbus on another voyage.

The Order from the Catholic Monarchs was that the expedition should be organised in ten days: three caravels provisioned, stored, ammunitioned, crewed, ready to sail. Impossible, but a better approach than any which might allow anything to be promised for tomorrow rather than be done today. At first, it appears (from witness evidence during a lawsuit many years later), recruitment of seamen was a main cause of delay for Columbus: 'They all thought that anyone who would sail with him was marked for death.'

But Palos in 1492 was not all that different from an English fishing village in modern times—a small community employing small vessels owned and crewed by a few families on a basis of blood relationship or close friendship, and sharing the profits of the ventures they made. Three such families of Palos—the Pinzóns, the Niños and the Quinteros—became backers of the project. According to a lawsuit witness, the most enthusi-

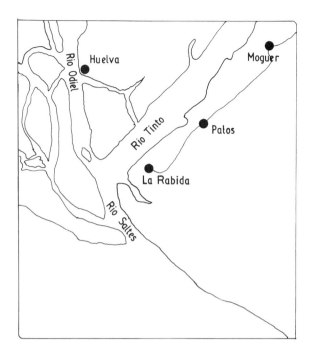

The area from which Columbus recruited his seamen for the first voyage. *Map drawn by Maurice Young*

astic was Martin Alonso Pinzón, who provided two caravels. He called a meeting of seafarers and told them: 'Come on, friends! Sail with us on this voyage. You will find houses with roofs of gold and win fame and fortune.'

As proof, he then produced a document which he said he had obtained from the Vatican library, describing a voyage from Spain to Cipangu made by the Queen of Sheba. With the alleged authority of the Pope's own library, this may have seemed confirmation of their hopes. Certainly, there were riches to be had out there to the west, and Pinzón was just as convinced of that as Columbus.

Naturally, there were sceptics. 'What about the Portuguese?' they objected. 'Many of them have sailed to the west, and what did they find? Nothing!' And there were enthusiasts and optimists to contradict. Pedro Vásquez de la Frontera was one who spoke up. He had sailed with just such a voyage of exploration in a Portuguese ship, he said, long ago. It was in 1452 and the name of the Portuguese navigator was Diogo de Teive. They had sailed out far beyond the Azores, to the south-west, until they reached an impenetrable barrier, thick beds of floating grass (which we call the Sargasso Sea). Then they had sailed north-east, hoping to find the legendary isle of Brazil, but had failed (although they had discovered the isle of Flores, the most westerly of the Azores archipelago). They had been driven as far north as the latitude of Ireland, and had then turned back. All his listeners should ship on this voyage with Columbus, he said; they would find a rich land.

After some weeks, the enthusiasts won their conflict with the sceptics and the timid; the community put its weight behind Columbus. The Royal Order for the venture to take place must have been one factor; the other was the hope of a share in the riches to be won by the voyage, as was customary then in such a community.

Palos, via the local shipping families, provided two of the required three caravels; the third vessel, owned by Juan de la Cosa, a Basque, was classed as a *nao*, which is merely Spanish for ship. Considering that these three are probably the most famous vessels in history, our lack of information about them is distressing. But where virtually all is speculation, perhaps guesswork is permissible.

Usually, vessels are classified by the form of their hulls, or the method of construction used, or the type of propulsion employed—in the case of a sailing craft this means how many masts, how many sails, how rigged, and so on.

The name 'caravel' may have an Arabic origin and certainly comes from southern Europe. Possibly, it may have derived from the use of carvel-type construction (the planks butted edge-to-edge rather than over-lapping as in clinker building). It is believed that the caravel type started as a fishing boat which, proving fast and handy, began to be built larger, to 50 tons or more. Pictures indicate that they were low hulled (thus offering little wind resistance), shallow-draught vessels with two masts carrying triangular lateen sails (the yards being fixed to the masts on the fore-and-aft line), as opposed to a ship-rigged vessel with 'square' sails. For reasons lost to us, the Portuguese explorers preferred the caravel to the ship-rigged vessel; but ability to sail close to the wind and to tack off a lee shore in shallow water must have been high on their list of priorities. For an Atlantic crossing, this ability would not be so important—until the vessels arrived off the islands of Cipangu. But you can't have everything. There is no perfect ship; there are only floating transport vehicles which do some jobs better than others.

Juan de la Cosa's *nao* was probably deeper hulled than the two caravels, more capacious, and if so would carry more of the stores necessary for so long a voyage into the unknown. Where they were going, there would be no European ports, no dockyards, no bases, not even a ship chandlers; the expedition must be completely self-contained.

The fleet contained less than 100 men, divided as follows between the three vessels:

Santa Maria
Juan de la Cosa's *nao*, with the owner himself aboard as master, was chosen as flagship. Her mariners' nickname was *La Gallega*, 'The Galician', since she was Basque in origin. Columbus sailed in her as captain-general

of the fleet. Peralonso Niño of Moguer was the pilot, Diego Chachu the boatswain. There was a surgeon, Juan Sǎnchez of Cordova; a steward, Pedro de Terreros; and a secretary, Rodrigo de Escobedo. A number of Royal officials travelled in the flagship, including Rodrigo Sanchez de Segovia, Pedro Gutiérrez of the Royal household, and Diego de Harana of Cordova, marshal (who was a cousin of Beatriz Enriques de Harana, Columbus's mistress). The task of the officials included checking the business side of the venture, as they expected to bring back much gold, silver, jewellery and spices. An interpreter was provided. He was Luis de Torres, a Christianised Jew who spoke Hebrew, Aramaic and Arabic. It was anticipated that in Cipangu and in India at least Arabic would be understood. In addition, there were another 30 or so men, some important, such as the carpenter, the master gunner, the cooper, the caulker, and various seamen, servants and ship's boys.

Santa Clara

A caravel owned by the Niño family of Palos and known to the seamen (and to history) as the *Nina*. Her owner, Juan Niño of Moguer, sailed in her as master under the command of Vicente Yáñez Pinzón of Palos. Sancho Ruis de Gama was her pilot; the surgeon was Master Alonso of Moguer. In addition, there were some 20 seamen as crew.

Pinta

A caravel belonging to Cristóbal Quintero of Palos, who also served in her as a seaman; her official name is not known. Unlike the *Nina*, which was lateen-rigged, the *Pinta* had a square-sail set-up. Two Pinzóns sailed in her—Martin Alonso as captain and Francisco Martin Pinzón as master. Cristóbal Garcia Xalmiento was the pilot, Juan Quintero of Palos the boatswain, Master Diego the surgeon, Garcia Fernández of Palos the steward. Plus some 20 seamen as crew.

This is virtually the limit of our certain knowledge from documents. We know that the flagship carried a master gunner, but what were her guns? And how were the caravels armed? In recent years systematic and careful excavation of wrecks has filled in some details, for the Institute of Nautical Archaeology of Texas A & M University has studied a number of ship remains dating to the early period of exploration (*c*. 1492–1522). Little or nothing of the hull, its fittings and its cargo had survived; the ballast, the anchors, and the armament proved to be the most enduring items.

One vessel had carried as main armament what the University call *bombardetas*. These were wrought-iron breech-loading guns about six feet long, firing a four-pound shot. Almost all early guns were of this type and in the larger sizes were originally called bombards (in English) from which we get the term bombardment and the Royal Artillery rank of bombardier. (Some North American authors tend to call them lombards, which incongruously invokes the inhabitants of the plain of Lombardy in Italy). Later, they developed specialisation, and in the English inventories which I have studied (mainly for the fleets of Henry VII and Henry VIII but also of Henry V and Elizabeth I) acquired a whole range of new names. In England, they are usually described as built-up guns (as opposed to cast pieces), the barrels being constructed with staves and hoops like a wine cask, which is how, in English, a gun barrel derived its name. But just to make things awkward for anyone seeking for embracing generalities, the first such gun I myself recovered from the Tudor battleship *Mary Rose* (1509–1545) proved to have a barrel made from a single rolled sheet welded along the seam and then strengthened with iron hoops shrunk on.

The secondary armament of the small ships of exploration examined by the Texas team consisted of swivel guns, some of which had been constructed in the very same way. Most authorities appear to agree that these are what the Spaniards referred to as a *verso*. The *Mary Rose* had them, too, in different sizes, the extant inventory classifying them under the heading *base*.

Unlike the muzzle-loading cannon with which most people are familiar, these barrels were simply a tube open at both ends. One end was the

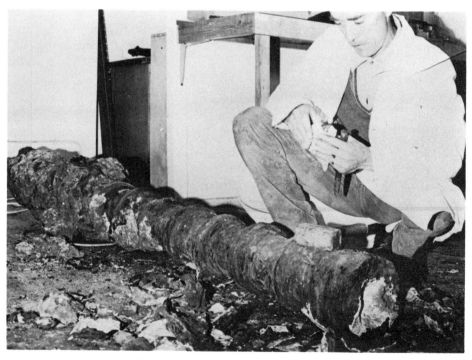

Wrought-iron breech-loading gun raised by the author from the *Mary Rose* in 1970, showing part of the natural concretion which had formed on it. The ships of Columbus were armed with long, thin guns like this, but smaller.

muzzle, the other was the 'hall' which took the shot and wadding; the gunpowder was contained in a separate 'chamber', so that re-loading was a simple process. The wrecks studied by Texas University held no surviving gun-carriages for the larger *bombardetas*. The *versos* and *bases*, of course, must have been rail-mounted guns, in calibre, though not perhaps in kick, roughly equivalent in modern times to the Boyes anti-tank rifle *c.* 1942, which was six feet long, weighed over 40 lbs, and fired a half-inch bullet (from the prone position). Even lying down, the firer was pushed a foot or more backwards by the recoil.

The wrecks also produced examples in the range of what we now call small arms: the arquebus and the crossbow. There must also have been edged cutting weapons such as swords and daggers and what are called pole arms—pikes, for instance.

Although not warships, for their size the ships of Columbus must have been well armed against whatever might be out there. But more mundane questions still require answers. Where did the crews sleep, for instance? And what did they eat, and how was it cooked? It has been suggested that, except for a few officers who had cabins, they all slept on deck. The commonsense answer is the palliasse, a crude mattress made out of a sack filled with straw.

The cooking may have been done on the upper deck on something like a modern barbecue arrangement. Perhaps, and then again maybe not. Admittedly, the *Mary Rose* was a battleship, with a normal complement of over 400 men, but she had a brick-lined galley down below with large copper cauldrons for cooking. The men who sailed out with Columbus and Pinzón and Niño would have had biscuit ('hard tack') instead of bread, and they would have had wine to drink.

Certainly, they regarded themselves as soldiers; indeed, Columbus later was to say so specifically. There was a certain amount of display. Although the lower hulls were black with pitch both to help keep them watertight and to deter the 'worm', the upper parts were bright with paint and the sails bore coloured devices; streamers and flags were flown. The heavier guns were stacked below, and some of the lighter ones also; they had a great ocean to cross—seaworthiness was all.

In the darkness half an hour before sunrise, on Friday, 3 August, 1492, the fleet sailed. They were not deliberately stealing away in the dark, they had to catch the tide farther down river. Where the River Saltés joined the Rio Tinto they saw a fourth ship, also waiting for the tide. The stranger carried a shipload of Jews, men and women who refused to accept Christianity and preferred exile. For a little while, the refugee ship kept company with them, then turned to the south-east, towards the Mediterranean, while Columbus and his fleet manoeuvred across the wind to the south-west, towards the Canary Islands.

43

5
The Last Landfall of All

The internal politics of the expedition are crucial to our understanding, could we but know them. That they existed is certain. As to their nature, we have only a statement by Columbus in his log, that the rudder-trouble which almost at once developed with the *Pinta* was due to sabotage.

Natural factions did exist and the prime task of Columbus, over-shadowing all others—even navigation—was to impose his ideas on everyone so that the fleet became a unit under his command: that is, on some 90 men divided between three vessels, voice communication being difficult.

There had been months of preparation, when the ships were being fitted out, stored and armed, for the various parties to get to know each other. The solid basis for the expedition lay in the ship-owning families, such as the Pinzóns, the Niños and the Quinteros, who supplied not just ships but many of the officers and seamen. It would be natural for them to regard themselves as the modern professionals and Columbus as something of an armchair amateur, having been away from the ocean so long. They might, however, be excessively impressed by his knowledge of world charts and the big names in geography and astronomy which he could drop. He had corresponded with Toscanelli, had he not? His book learning was immense. And, of course, there was his influence at Court and there were Court officials travelling with him in the *Santa Maria*.

Certainly, the Pinzóns were in agreement with his basic ideas: not to try the north part of the North Atlantic, where the seas were icy and the winds keen and dead foul for any ship trying to make headway to the west. Go south to the Canaries before turning west. And if Columbus said that Cipangu was at the same 'height' on the globe as the Canaries, he probably knew best; in that case, a straight run out would mean eventually an arrival at the Japanese islands, after travelling some 2,600 miles according to the calculations of Columbus.

One ship owner at least had doubts. This was Cristóbal Quintero, owner of the caravel *Pinta* commanded by Martin Alonso Pinzón. According to the log of Columbus, both Quintero and a colleague, Gómez Rascón, had shown signs of defeatism during the time of preparation, complaining and finding excuses for being unready to sail. The services of both the caravels, it will be recalled, had been forced by the Court as a fine for smuggling by the mariners and shippers of Palos. One of the Quintero family, Juan, went in her as boatswain, but her owner, Cristóbal, served in her only as a seaman. That is odd and unexplained.

But certainly, there must have been pessimists in all three crews, men who thought: All very well to sail with steady winds to the west, but if the winds stay like that, how do we get back? Do we tack to and fro until we starve? Or, more likely, perish of thirst?

And, equally certain, the captains of all three ships must have agreed between themselves to practise a deliberate deception of their men.

Columbus admits it in his log. Each day's run would be totalled correctly in the log, but a lesser figure for that day's sailing would be given out to the men. The log, of course, had to be correct—or as accurate as they could get it—because the navigation depended on it. Logs and charts were working documents. If, say, the true figure for 24 hours' sailing was 150 miles, then Columbus might announce 141. And so, he and the other captains calculated, their men would not be so oppressed by the thought of the steady following wind which blew them farther and farther from their homes.

Shortly after leaving Palos on 3 August, the ships had passed the monastery of Santa Maria de la Rabida on its cliff overlooking the estuary. Here Columbus had received friendly help and encouragement early in the bitter years of pleading, when few would listen. Now his enterprise was fully launched at last, he was leaving them behind. The representatives of the monarchs were with him in the *Santa Maria*, part of his seaborne staff, but apart from them he was on his own.

Nor were the first few days trouble-free. No doubt, few expected that they would be. Ships and crews have to be 'worked up', small faults ironed out, problems met and corrected, the men welded together gradually so that at length they will work almost without command, knowing instinctively what has to be done. But not at first. And especially not under a new commander.

To start with, the caravels were faster and handier than the *nao*. Built in the Basque country, the *Santa Maria* was probably a North Atlantic ship, built high at bow and stern to cope with the heavy, immense deep seas of that region. But certainly she was slow, comparatively speaking, if a later average of about 100 miles a day can be considered dawdling.

The caravel *Nina*, with her lateen rig, sailed well; but when the winds freshened and then blew from all quarters, the rig was harder to control than the square sails of the *Pinta* and the *Santa Maria*.

Then on the fourth day out from Palos, the *Pinta*'s rudder became unshipped, so that she was left wallowing in the rough seas. How this happened is not clear, but Columbus wrote in the log his belief that it had

45

been the result of deliberate action by the owners, Cristóbal Quintero, and Gómez Rascón, in order to abort the voyage. The rudder would have been hung on the sternpost by a system of pintles and gudgeons (such as may be seen on old-fashioned rowing boats today), and might have been awkward to sabotage while actually at sea. If sabotage it was, then Quintero would have had the best chance of doing the damage while the vessel still lay at Palos, for who would question the owner's right to fuss around his own ship?

Columbus brought the *Santa Maria* as close alongside the *Pinta* as he dared, shouted words of encouragement to her crew, and was relieved to find that her captain, Martin Alonso Pinzón, was fixing a temporary repair of the rudder connection with ropes. Columbus praised Martin Alonso for his intelligence and resourcefulness—and this is the first and the last praise of Pinzón in the log. Perhaps they shortly afterwards became rivals, competitors for the same prize, rather than dissenters who wanted to give up right at the start and abort the entire project. In any event, the makeshift repair did not last. After making 87 miles the rope fastenings of the rudder broke. Columbus now had to do something drastic or see his

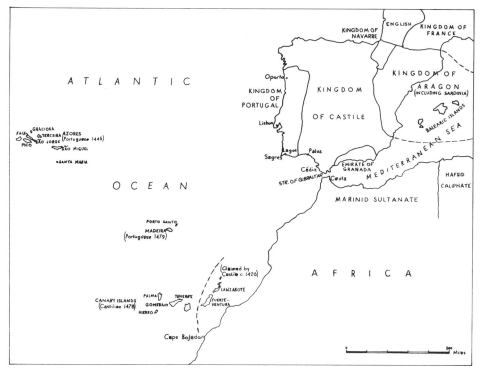

Spain and Portugal in relation to the Canaries, Madeira and the Azores. *Map drawn by Maurice Young*

whole enterprise fatally weakened. Three ships he must have, and if the *Pinta* let him down, then he must replace her with a locally hired vessel.

Martin Pinzón sought a less drastic and impatient solution. He wanted to make for the nearest large island of the Canaries group, Lanzarote, and effect proper repairs there. Columbus over-ruled him. He told Pinzón to head for the isle of Gran Canaria, and if permanent repairs were not possible, then another ship must be obtained, and the *Pinta* left behind.

Both Columbus and Pinzón were forced to guess at what resources might be available at the various islands of the group held by Spain. Fighting between the natives and the Spaniards had been going on until a few months before on La Palma and, having subdued that island, the Governor-General, the adventurer Alonso de Lugo, was planning to attack the formidable volcanic island of Tenerife, where a race of giant natives, the Guanches, were to put up desperately effective resistance for some years. The Canaries represented the farthest outpost of Spain, an embattled frontier zone before the unknown wastes of ocean.

Columbus did have one source of local knowledge. During his time at Court he had met the beautiful young widow of Gomera, Beatriz de Peraza y Bobadilla, who had been appointed maid of honour to Queen Isabella after her adulterous husband, the Governor, had been slain in a native uprising. Gomera was almost the last island of the Canary group which he would leave behind him when he sailed out to the west; the last opportunity to re-victual, water, and take on wood for the galley fires. To call at Gomera would be sound planning in any case, but there was to be one witness, a friend who knew him well, who suspected that he loved the lady.

The *Santa Maria* and *Nina* escorted the crippled *Pinta* to Gran Canaria. Once there, Columbus told Pinzón that he was going on to Gomera with the *Santa Maria* and *Nina*, to see if any suitable replacement ship was there; and if there was not, that he would return to Gran Canaria with both vessels to help with the *Pinta*'s repairs.

There seemed to be a jinx on the voyage. Instead of a swift passage to Gomera, Columbus met contrary winds or calms. He did not reach the island until Sunday, 12 August; he anchored and sent a boat ashore. The islanders were famous for being able to whistle coded messages (rather like bird song) over great distances, but that was of no use to Columbus. When eventually the boat returned, the news was exasperatingly contrary. Doña Beatriz was away, visiting Gran Canaria—the very place he had just come from. On the other hand, the 40-ton ship she was using, from description seemed ideal as a possible replacement for the *Pinta*.

Columbus lay at anchor off Gomera for several days, rightly impatient to be away but compelled to bide his time. The sailing season was half over; what he did not know was that, where he was going, there was a hurricane season due—winds of around 100 m.p.h and waves 50 feet high. In the eternal springtime of the Canaries that would have been difficult to visualise. The height of the sun at mid-day told them they were in the same latitude as Cipangu was said to be; at mid-day, a man threw hardly any shadow, for the sun was almost directly above. The cities of the Great Khan, the buildings with roofs of gold, might be only just down below the horizon.

On 15 August Columbus learned that a small vessel was due to sail for Gran Canaria. It was Spanish, of course; the natives owned no ships, had never learnt how to build a boat even, so each group had remained cut off from all the others, each community imprisoned on its separate island. That was a mystery, for how had they got there in the first place?

Columbus decided to aid Pinzón by sending him a specialist from his own crew, who could help repair the *Pinta*, and he penned a note for the man to take to her captain. He would have come himself, he wrote, had the *Santa Maria* not been such a bad sailer. But he was waiting in the harbour of Gomera and they were all anxiously expecting Pinzón's arrival there.

Next day the *Santa Maria* still swung to her anchor, and Columbus noted in the log, 'Still no sign of Doña Beatriz.' The last time they had met, he had been a supplicant at the court of the two monarchs; now he had his own small kingdom, his vindication just over the horizon; and she was governing this frontier island in her dead husband's place.

One more day, and on 17 August Columbus was recording that it was now two weeks since they had set out from Palos, that the crew were growing restive, and that he had become very worried for the safety of Doña Beatriz. And why was there still no sign of Martin Pinzón?

Unable to stand inaction, Columbus went ashore to see if he personally could find some ship suitable to replace the *Pinta*, but of course there was nothing. There were hardly any vessels available, certainly none capable of voyages across open water. He steeled himself to accept that he was powerless, but the following day a special mass was said on board for the safe return of the lady of Gomera, Doña Beatriz, and for Martin Pinzón. Columbus decided to wait three more days before sailing back with both ships to Gran Canaria, where Pinzón must be and Doña Beatriz should be.

By 24 August, three weeks had passed since leaving Spain, and two of those weeks quite wasted. The waiting and the sense of things going wrong worried the crew; sailing back the way they had come did not make them any happier. But worse was in store. They had weighed anchor at dawn on the 24th and by mid-day they had sighted the vessel which had left Gomera on the 15th with Columbus's message for Pinzón and the man who was to help him with the repair. For a whole week this ship had met contrary winds and had made virtually no progress. The implications for their return voyage, when they had sailed down wind thousands of miles

The Bay of San Sebastian, Gomera. The church where Columbus worshipped still stands among the modern buildings. *Courtesy Spanish National Tourist Office*

past Gomera, were plain. Plain that is, to anyone not privy to Columbus's sailing plan of picking up the westerly winds in the North Atlantic for the return passage. 'Plan' is perhaps not the right word: thus far, it was merely a theory—but all their lives depended upon it.

From the south-western coast of Tenerife you can see Gomera, a small, lumpy island only a few miles away. Tenerife is much larger and higher, basically a mountain ridge rising out of the sea, capped by the volcanic cone of the Pico de Teide 12,152 feet (3,717 metres) high. Often the peak is not visible, because of a cloud layer halfway up the slope, cold and moist. The cone is an active volcano thrust up out of an old crater many miles across, to be known (after its capture in 1496) as Las Cañadas. The *Santa Maria* and the *Nina* spent the night lying off Tenerife, and the volcano

Las Cañadas del Teide: the floor of the old volcanic crater below Teide on the island of Tenerife in the Canaries. The cloud-covered peak can be glimpsed in the background.
Courtesy Spanish National Tourist Office

50

chose that night to erupt. The uncanny glare from the glowing fields of lava flowing down the slopes, the noise, the spectacle of fire and smoke and explosion, the sheer power that could rift the mountain and shake the earth, was intimidating, perhaps an omen to those who had never seen such a spectacle before. Columbus, who had seen Etna red over Sicily, had to explain what a volcano was and to describe some of those he knew from his earlier seafaring.

The next island to the eastward was Gran Canaria, and they reached it by nine in the morning. They had no trouble in finding the *Pinta*, but it disturbed Columbus to see that the rudder was not repaired even now. He was convinced that the reluctance of the ship's owner, Cristóbal Quintero, and his henchman Gómez Rascón, to make the great voyage was the cause. He did not accept the excuse that Gran Canaria, captured from its neolithic inhabitants only ten years before, lacked port facilities. Enquiring closer, he found that Juan Pérez Viscaino had recaulked the caravel and completely cured her leaks. That made the *Pinta* a much better proposition and he decided that the best thing to do was to have a new rudder constructed, rather than botch up the old one, and set the *Santa Maria*'s boatswain, Diego Chachu, to organise this work.

In a flurry of decision, he also ordered that the *Nina* should have a major alteration to her rig, from lateen to square sails, because these were more efficient when driven by a steady following wind, as they would be, particularly on the return passage across the North Atlantic in the band of westerly winds which he had noted off the coasts of Portugal, Galicia and England.

He also learned that Doña Beatriz had sailed from Gran Canaria, bound for Gomera, five days earlier; how they had missed each other was inexplicable. Columbus consoled himself with the thought that God must have planned it that way. Otherwise, he argued to himself, if he had exchanged the *Pinta* for her ship, yet more time would have been wasted in transferring the stores from one to the other. As it was, they had been delayed two weeks and had consumed two weeks' supply of food, earmarked for the voyage. He had allowed for that by leaving behind on Gomera a wood, water and foraging party under Pedro Gutiérrez, an officer of the Royal household.

He had a dozen men requisitioning and storing food on Gomera under the experienced Gutiérrez, a group of carpenters working on the new rudder for the *Pinta* under Diego Chachu, and, despite his initial objections, the captain of the *Nina*, Vincente Yáñez Pinzón, was now convinced and working with determination and skill to re-rig his caravel. And, of course, the caulking party under Juan Pérez Viscaino had made the leaky *Pinta* watertight. Columbus was careful to give credit to all the key men in his team.

At mid-day on 31 August the work on the *Pinta*'s rudder was completed, and that afternoon the three ships hauled their anchors and got under way for Gomera. With a fresh breeze and the cold Canaries current flowing south-west, they made good time. Columbus may have known about the Canaries current; but no one could know what the circulation pattern was farther out. That it followed the wind pattern, becoming warm before it turned back north-east towards Scotland, was to be a bonus, but Columbus could never have counted on it. He was sure only of the wind pattern because he had experienced that—or at any rate, part of it, deducing the rest.

On 1 September they were at Gomera. Columbus says he met many fine, trustworthy Spaniards there, but mentioned one only by name, Doña Beatriz de Peraza y Bobadilla, the governor. He was now very optimistic, because he was meeting people who swore that every year, from time to time, land was seen out to the west, almost in line with the setting sun. This was confirmation of a story already known to Columbus: in 1484 a Portuguese mariner had asked the King for a caravel to go to just such another land lying far out in the ocean to the west. Then, as he well knew from his years there, people in the Azores told the same story of on occasion sighting an unknown land far out to sea.

Now, at last, he had the men and the means to go out and search. The outward journey, he thought, should take no more than three weeks' sailing; but to allow for contrary winds or currents, it would be best to have a reserve of seven days. Four weeks' supplies in all, therefore. He passed this order on to Gutiérrez, who had already assembled stores of salt, wine, molasses and honey and was now busy collecting supplies of dried meat, salted fish and fruits. The latter would have to be issued at once, before they went bad. The biscuit should be ready for loading in a day or two. Considering that Gomera lacked the facilities for ship supply found in Spain and Portugal—the Portuguese were particularly good at provisioning ships—he could have no complaint about the help he had had from the Spaniards of Gomera. As for the return voyage, Columbus had no doubt that the fine harbours of Cipangu or Cathay could supply all the provisions he needed.

At sunrise on Thursday, 6 September, a special service of thanksgiving was held, for everything was now ready. But before they could sail, bad news came in, carried by the captain of a caravel arriving from the island of Hierro, which the Portuguese called Ferro.*

---

* The most westerly island of the Canaries group, the last land Columbus would pass on his way west, was in 1630 declared by a scientific conference assembled in Paris to be the first meridian of longitude, 0 degree. The alternative and rival meridian of Greenwich, in the capital of England, was not universally accepted until late in the nineteenth century.

The alarming news he brought was that a squadron of three Portuguese caravels was cruising to the west, apparently with orders to intercept Columbus and prevent his voyage of exploration. Columbus thought that this conjecture might be true, for King John II of Portugal might well be angry that he had gone over to Castile. (Alternatively, the Portuguese may have suspected that the Columbus expedition was aimed at their route to the Gold Coast and the Cape of Good Hope.)

Although Columbus left harbour promptly before noon on 6 September, he was soon becalmed in the narrow channel between Gomera and the barren landscape of Tenerife's south-west shore. On 8 September, however, the north-easterly breeze he had counted on started to blow, and the little force began to move away to the south-west. This showed up yet another defect in the *Santa Maria*—she plunged her bows deep into the waves and took a good deal of water on board, so much so that Columbus had to shorten sail. The fault did not recur apparently, so presumably Columbus had ballast or cargo restowed to make the *nao* lie deeper at the stern.

On Sunday, 9 September, they had completely lost sight of land. Not even the 12,000-feet high peak of Tenerife was visible. All around them was the blue ocean, miles deep, and the blue sky, miles high.

6
Stella Maris Misleads

Most of the men must have known with fair accuracy how long the provisions would last. They might not have been told that Columbus had ordered the ships to be provisioned for 28 days, hoping to make the Indies in 21, but many of them would have handled the stores aboard, both at Palos and at Gomera; and they had left Gomera on Thursday, 6 September, at noon. So that was Day One. Day Two would begin at noon on the following day. And that day was wasted; they were becalmed and made no progress.

Sunday, 9 September, was Day Four. This was the day when at last there was no land in sight: neither behind them, nor ahead. From now on they were entering the unknown. No man born had been here before them.

Few were volunteers. Most had taken up the sea to make a living, in preference perhaps to toil on the land or in some indoor trade; they had been ordered to come on this voyage. They heartily desired to survive it.

That day, in daylight they covered 15 leagues, but Columbus announced a lesser distance 'so that the crews should not lose heart if the voyage grew too long'. During the hours of darkness he reckoned that they had gone 120 Roman miles farther, at 10 Roman miles an hour, making 30 leagues covered in the 24 hours from mid-day to mid-day. He noted that the helmsmen steered badly, falling off from their intended course of due west somewhat to the north, and he had to check them for it.

The bulk of the crew were divided into working groups or 'watches', being on duty for eight hours at a time; so the groups would be changed three times in every 24 hours. The time was kept by means of a half-hour sandglass placed beside the compass on the poop, with a duty boy always in attendance to turn it when the sand had run through. It was his duty also to call the next watch to get ready, shortly before the sand ran out at the end of a watch. There was a trick of warming the glass with the hands, to make the sand run faster; and as an error here would affect the navigational calculations, any offender caught was severely punished.

The men on lookout duty, probably one at the bow and another in the 'top', a bucket-like affair high up the main mast, had vital tasks: not merely to look ahead and around for land, but to note possible signs of it—drifting tree branches or wreckage, drifting weed, the flight of birds and their type (often a clue to land), the cloud formations (also a clue to land), the colour of the sea which could indicate deep water or shallows, and even the smell of land. The only definite, measurable indication of depth was a lump of lead attached to a line. The line itself might not be marked but could—and can—be measured in the traditional way by holding each length as it comes back inboard between outstretched arms, which equals some six feet (and in English is called a 'fathom', in Spanish a *brazo*). The 'lead' itself had a hollow bottom packed with tallow, which would pick up samples of the seabed if it was sand, shingle, shell, mud or clay. In coastal navigation these were important clues to position, especially when in fog. Out in the Atlantic, where depths are measured in miles, the lead and line were useless. Anchoring was also impossible.

Monday, 10 September was Day Five. Columbus reckoned that they made 60 leagues at 10 Roman miles an hour (8 knots in modern usage) but announced that they had come only 48 leagues. This consistent faking of the distances run every day seems to show Columbus's lack of confidence in his crews (and their lack of confidence in him). Columbus's own private record of those distances was only an estimate, in any case.

The courses steered were by the compass (similar to a modern boat's or diver's compass, but somewhat different in use from that of an aeroplane). In this case, Columbus was trying to steer due west along the imaginary line connecting the Canaries with Cipangu, his compass being subject to exactly the same errors as modern compasses of the same type (i.e., not gyro). Deviation caused by metal objects near the compass (guns, anchors, iron ballast, etc.) is one cause of error which would have been well known to him; but the error which today we call variation was probably not known at the time, at least in its full complexity.

The compass he was using was basically a magnetised needle attached to a circular card, balanced on a thin brass point so that it was free to revolve and point to the north—in principle no different from the modern magnetic compass.

But what the compass needle points to is not geographical north but a large magnetic anomaly, inconstant in position, which today lies between the geographical North Pole and Canada. So the error varies according to where you happen to be on the globe's surface at the relevant time (and if you were in a certain part of Canada, the magnetic pole would be in line with the geographical pole, and no error would be apparent).

In modern times there is no real problem for navigators because the errors are known and can be allowed for. They are marked on aviation maps and nautical charts. But the changing variations must have been unknown to Columbus and were not marked on his charts (which were no more than crude speculations inevitable before anyone had actually entered these unknown regions). To give some idea of the unguessed-at complexities of the errors, I have picked out four charts from my own collection.

The first three cover much the same area of southern England south of London. The first in date and of practical use is Ordnance Survey Aviation Map Sheet 11 of 1934. Marked on it is the current Variation Error for that area: 11° 50′ West with annual change 11′ Easterly. The second is British Admiralty chart No 2045, Christchurch to Owers, of 1959, with the current Variation Error marked as 8° 35′ West decreasing about 8′ annually. The third is British Admiralty chart No 394, The Solent Eastern Part, of 1974, with the current Variation Error marked as 7° 05′ West, decreasing about 4′ annually. The last chart would have interested Columbus very much. It is British Admiralty chart No 3251 of 1969, for the area Islas Canarias to Cap Blanc. The Variation Error is shown as 12° 40′ West decreasing 8′ annually and there is a note against the isle of La Palma, north of Gomera: 'Local Magnetic Anomaly (see Caution No 1).' The latter acknowledges that this chart is based mainly on French and Spanish charts of 1933–64. Armed with this information, a navigator cannot go far wrong (assuming that his compass is corrected for deviation error as much as possible and that any remaining discrepancies are known and can be allowed for).

But a navigator in 1492 was in no such position. Worse still, he had no really accurate means of time-keeping or of measuring speed through the water: a half-hour glass and a log line must have been highly approximate. Then there was the additional error due to wind drift and another caused by the set of the currents. Columbus should have made good a track many degrees away from the desired due west. But we can see that he did not. He steered straight for Japan, the half-mythical Cipangu of Marco Polo, where the land of spices and treasure awaited him. How did he do it?

The way to check by natural means any variation error existing is by comparing the North Star, Stella Maris, with compass north; and from a ship's deck, especially with fifteenth-century instruments—quadrant or astrolabe—this would not be easy. And there was one more error, as yet unsuspected, lying in wait to trip the navigator five centuries ago.

In general terms, the compass, the stars and the sun were more reliable than modern instruments for direction and position finding; they were not subject to electrical failure, for instance. At the time, however, the newly invented compass represented high technology. As the poet Guiot de Provins wrote in AD 1206:

Through the magnet, an ugly brown stone to which iron turns of its own accord, mariners possess an art that cannot fail them. A needle touched by it and floated by a stick on water turns its point to the pole star, and a light being placed near the needle on dark nights, the proper course is known.

The stars and the sun also were reliable instruments for position finding on the globe of earth. If Columbus was sailing along the equator, he would know it because the Pole Star would be touching the horizon, whereas if he sailed north to the Canaries the Pole Star would be 29° above the horizon, and if he was approaching southern Spain or Portugal, the height of the Pole Star would be 37°. By keeping the height of the Pole Star constant at 29° he could travel round the world on the same latitude as the Canaries.

Another check was familiar to everyone since the work of Claudius Ptolemy in the second century AD, which showed that a stake driven into the ground at Alexandria casts a longer shadow than an identical stake similarly driven into the earth some 1,000 miles to the south at Syené. Ptolemy measured the lengths cast by the two stakes, and knowing the distance between the two points of measurement, calculated the diameter of the globe. His result did not accord with that of Columbus—but the principle was clear. By measuring shadows on the ship when the sun was at its highest, one had a solar check on Polaris the north star; and also on the compass and any estimates of drift or current tending to take the ship off the desired course of due west.

None of this would work without long experience behind the navigator. The computer was his own mind, into which were fed all these observable factors, plus half a lifetime's experience in judging wind and current and speed through the water to reach an uncannily accurate result.

Day Six was 11 September, which brought a reminder of the mariner's mortality—the little squadron passed part of the mast of a 120-ton ship, lapped by waves far out from land. This day and every day, Columbus kept the two reckonings—the real one and the spurious one showing a lesser distance covered to the west than he calculated was really the case. On checking the *Santa Maria*'s compasses (there were more than one, probably at least three) Columbus noted an odd thing. That night the needles of all the compasses pointed to the west of the Pole Star, but in the pre-dawn of the next day had returned to a heading slightly east of Stella Maris.

Day Nine. The crew of the *Nina* reported having seen a tern and a tropic-bird. Columbus noted: neither can go more than 25 leagues from land.

Day Ten. They covered more than 27 leagues to the west. Early that night they saw a flaming portent in the sky, which streaked down to hit the sea four or five leagues distant from the ships. Columbus noted it as a marvellous spectacle, but according to Bartholomé Las Casas, the author of *Historia de las Indias*, the crews took the sign for an omen of ill-fortune for the voyage.

Day Eleven. Little clouds appeared and rode with the wind which was driving the ships westward. The weather became mild and temperate. The

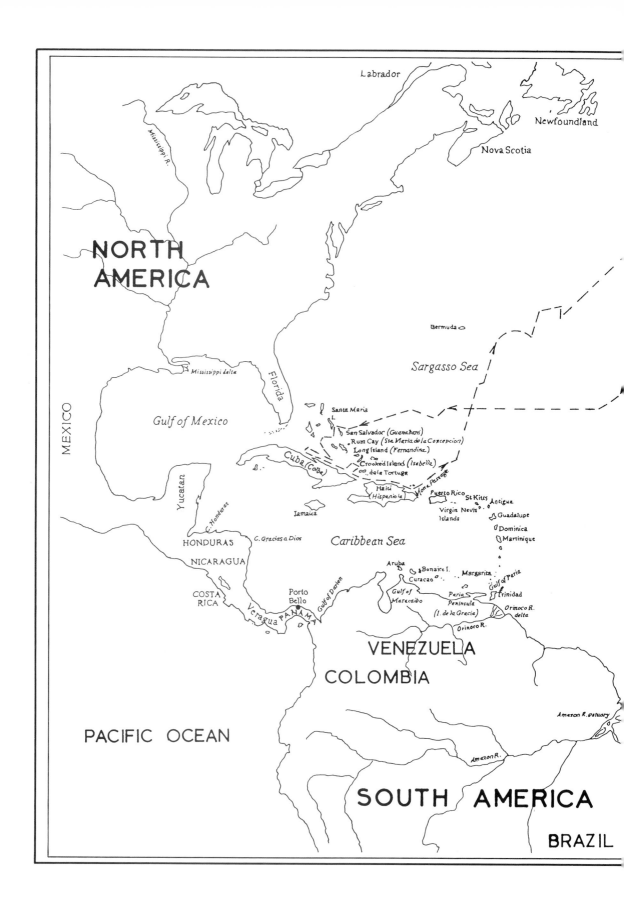

Labrador

Newfoundland

Nova Scotia

Mississippi R.

NORTH
AMERICA

Bermuda

Sargasso Sea

Mississippi delta

Florida

MEXICO

Gulf of Mexico

Santa Maria

San Salvador (Guanahani)
Rum Cay (Sta. Maria de la Concepcion)
Long Island (Fernandina)
Crooked Island (Isabella)
de la Tortuga

Cuba (Cuba)

B.

Mona Passage

Puerto Rico   St Kitts   Antigua
Virgin   Nevis
Islands

Haiti
(Hispaniola)

Jamaica

Guadalupe

Dominica

Martinique

C. Honduras

Yucatan

HONDURAS

C. Gracias a Dios

Caribbean Sea

NICARAGUA

Aruba
Bonaire I.
Curacao

Margarita

Gulf of Paria

COSTA
RICA

Porto
Bello

Gulf of Darien

Gulf of
Maracaibo

Paria
Peninsula
(I. de la Grecia)

Trinidad

Veragua   PANAMA

Orinoco R.
delta

Orinoco R.

VENEZUELA

COLOMBIA

PACIFIC OCEAN

Amazon R. estuary

Amazon R.

SOUTH AMERICA

BRAZIL

Map drawn by Maurice Young

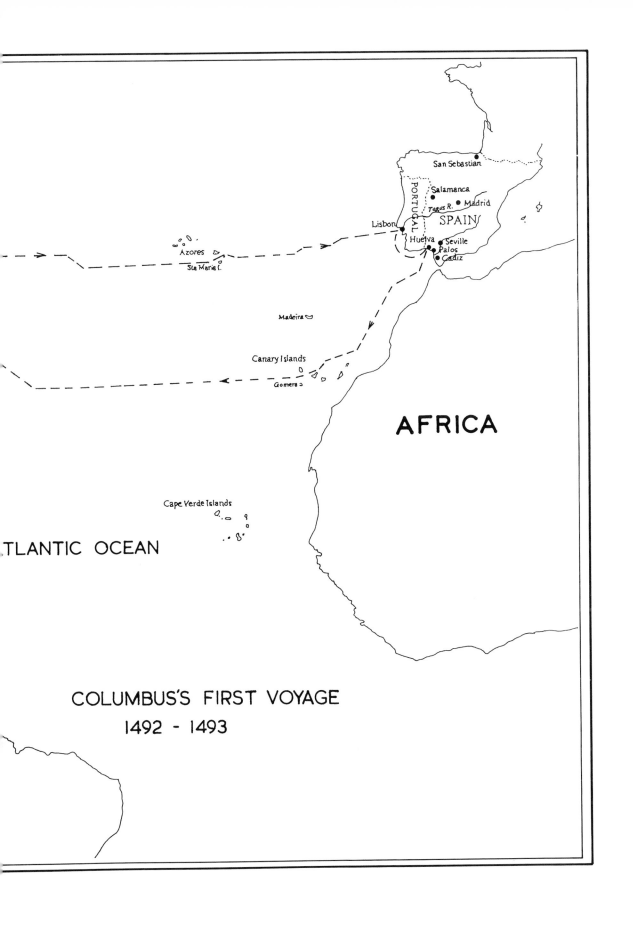

San Sebastian

PORTUGAL

Salamanca

Tagus R. • Madrid

SPAIN

Lisbon

Huelva

Seville

Palos

Cadiz

Azores

Sta Maria I.

Madeira

Canary Islands

Gomera

AFRICA

Cape Verde Islands

ATLANTIC OCEAN

COLUMBUS'S FIRST VOYAGE
1492 - 1493

mornings especially were delightful, 'like April in Andalusia'. This pleasant, almost dreamlike progress, as if between the banks of some warm river of southern Spain, was to continue day after day. These were the trade winds, not yet so called. An even more welcome event was the spectacle of drifting seaweed, apparently uprooted only recently. This convinced the mariners that the ships must be passing near an island. Columbus, however, having kept a careful (and confidential) reckoning of the distances run each day, did not believe that this could be Cipangu or Cathay. 'I think the mainland must be somewhat farther away.'

Then there appeared ahead a great mass of weed, thickly packed, blocking their path. Unlike land grass, sea plants do not have roots; their equivalent is the holdfast which grips rock or boulders or large stones. The mariners knew this, and read the spectacle as evidence of rocky shallows. No living man had seen the floating weedfields we know now as the Sargasso Sea (from the Portuguese *Sargaço*, a small grape resembling the flotation bladders of the weed) which is held in the centre of the North Atlantic by the circular pattern of the ocean currents.

The ships drove on before the trade winds and the mariners could see that the weed was not in fact continuous and could be pushed aside; nonetheless they found this strange phenomenon dispiriting.

Day Twelve. Columbus reckoned that they covered 50 leagues this day and gave out that it was only 47. The current was still with them, as they sailed with the wind behind, effortlessly. They were still in the midst of the weed sea. Columbus insisted that as it was very fine, it must have grown on rocks originally and these rocks must lie ahead. If so, they must be near land, possibly only an island, not worth searching for.

After dark, something strange happened again. The pilots took a bearing on Stella Maris, the Pole Star, and found that the compass no longer pointed to it, but to the north-west a full point. This additional uncertainty caused much dejection, although no one could cite a valid reason. It was just that they had left a known world for the unknown.

Columbus ordered the pilots to take another reading on the Pole Star at dawn—and this time there was no sudden discrepancy! Once more, the needle pointed directly at the faint star. Columbus pronounced the night's error to have been the fault of Stella Maris, not of the reliable compass. The Pole Star must change its position, he concluded: a bold verdict indeed when the difficulties of taking stellar observations from a ship's deck are understood, and for which Columbus has been mocked. But he was right: the Pole Star does indeed rotate around the geographical North Pole, only by about 1° now, but 3° 27' in the time of Columbus.

In the morning, they found a live crab living on the floating weed, and Columbus kept it as proof that land must be near.

Day Thirteen. They travelled more than 55 leagues but Columbus admitted to only 48. The sea was as smooth as some great river. Martin Pinzón, commanding the fast caravel *Pinta*, passed the *Santa Maria*, calling out to the Admiral that he had seen a great flock of birds flying to the west and that, with luck, he hoped to sight land that night. From the *Santa Maria*, a massed cloudbank appeared on the northern horizon. Yet another sign of land, thought Columbus.

Day Fourteen brought light winds and they covered only 25 leagues, Columbus admitting to 22. He noted repeated signs of the nearness of land—a booby bird (a species of gannet) in the morning, another in the evening, and a drizzle without any wind. He was sorely tempted, and so it seems were some of the crew, to go in search of it, but he told them, 'There is plenty of time. If God wills we shall see all this on our return voyage.' The navigators of the three vessels separately calculated the distance they had come from the Canaries. The *Nina*'s pilot made it 440 leagues, the pilot of the *Pinta* 420, and that of the *Santa Maria* 400. This was encouraging, as a navigational check, because it was the approximate distance out from the Canaries of the famed but never-found island of Antilia, according to the calculations of the cosmographer Toscanelli whom Columbus esteemed highly, and whose chart he was using.

Paolo Toscanelli, the Florentine cosmographer whose theories influenced Columbus and whose chart he carried on the first voyage.

Nowadays there is uncertainty about the modern measurement represented by the fifteenth-century Spanish or Portuguese league. Some think it represents 3.18 nautical miles, others 3.43. As a nautical mile is longer than our statute mile, it may be convenient to think of a league as being about 3½ land miles. If so, then the three vessels had sailed some 1,500 miles since parting from Doña Beatriz at Gomera on 6 September.

20 September was the fifteenth day out from Gomera. Two weeks had passed since they had completed storing and provisioning for a three-week voyage, with an allowance of an extra week's rations for safety's sake. This was the halfway mark before their supplies ran out. And now the winds were light and variable. They made only seven or eight leagues to the west. Columbus began to see increasing signs of approaching land: three booby birds; much seaweed; a 'river bird like a tern' which they caught; and yet another booby—'these birds sleep on land,' he noted. 'They go to sea in the morning in search of food and never fly more than 20 miles from land.' That was a guess. No one really knew. But it seemed likely.

Next day it was still calm with a little wind in the evening. Columbus logged 13 leagues as the distance run, but the track westward was shorter; they could not sail this day in a straight line either. But still he saw reassuring signs: a 'sea as smooth as a river, the air is the best in the world.' And a whale was sighted. 'Whales always keep close to land.'

Day Seventeen was 22 September, again with headwinds, so that they had to tack, progressing in zig-zags. But even an unfavourable wind could be regarded as helpful by Columbus. He noted that a wind blowing towards Spain helped calm the fears of his men that they were sailing into regions from which they could never return.

But next day they were fearful again, although reassuring signs of land were noted (by Columbus): a dove, a small 'river bird', some white birds, much seaweed with some crabs in it. What worried the crew was the strange smoothness of the sea, the stillness and calm of it. Where was the wind that might take them back to Spain?

Then an uncanny thing happened. In a flat calm, with no wind at all, the sea rose up and swelled into immense, broad waves. The men were amazed at the power of it. Of course, they realised that it was evidence of some tremendous wind many hundreds of miles away. When such things happen on a coast and a perfectly quiet sea swells up in dead silence and overflows the shore, smashing fences and even tearing down walls, it is hard to believe the evidence of one's eyes. Columbus wrote that nothing like this had been seen since the Jews came out of Egypt and murmured against Moses, who had led them out of bondage. The parallel was obvious.

All through this period there was constant angry grumbling from the

Martin Alonso Pinzón, Captain
of the caravel *Pinta. Courtesy
Arxiu MAS, Barcelona*

men. There was even a suggestion that Columbus should be thrown overboard, the course reversed, and the authorities back home presented with a story that the accident had occurred while Columbus was taking a reading of the stars.

Columbus does not say so, but he may have reduced the rations at around this time. It would have been a reasonable precaution, despite his optimism. The murmuring, the disquiet, cannot have been confined entirely to the crew of the flagship, for on Day Twenty Columbus noted that he had talked to Martin Alonso Pinzón, captain of the caravel *Pinta*, about a chart which he had sent over to him three days before, when the murmurings in his own ship were at their height. On the chart, certain islands were marked along their course across the Atlantic to Cathay. These, of course, could be sources of re-supply, where their stores of food and water might be topped up for a long voyage. Pinzón had thought that the fleet must now be in the vicinity of these islands, indeed should already have sighted them. Columbus agreed. The failure to sight the islands could be due to two things—that the currents (on which there could be no check) had carried them all to the north-east of their desired track, and that the pilots' calculations of distance run from the Canaries were too great. When this chart was sent back to the flagship on a line,

Columbus made considerable show of fixing their position on it, with the help of the *Santa Maria*'s pilot and members of the crew.

Possibly this was Toscanelli's chart, being used as a public relations exercise to calm the crew. By now, Columbus had many years' experience of how to convince doubters by means of visual, apparently scientific documentary evidence.

The magic worked once more, and at sunset they saw Pinzón on the poop of the *Pinta*, shouting across the water to Columbus that he had sighted land, and so claimed the reward.

Columbus sank to his knees and said a thankful prayer. In Pinzón's caravel *Pinta*, captain and crew joined in saying the *Gloria in Excelsis Deo*, in the *Santa Maria* they did the same. In the *Nina*, the crew swarmed up the masts and rigging, staring at the far horizon and calling excitedly to each other that they could certainly see land. Now Columbus himself could see it too. It was about 25 leagues away, he thought, more than a day's good sailing. He ordered the course changed to south-west, towards the land, which continued to be in sight until darkness came. As the first to sight it, Pinzón would receive the Royal gift of an annual pension of 10,000 *maravedis*.

In the morning it was calm and the sea very smooth. Many of the seamen went for a swim in the clear blue water, miles deep, cleansing themselves of ship-grime. The ships were followed by dolphins and fish.

It was now 26 September, and the end of the three weeks which, Columbus had calculated, should bring them to Cipangu or Cathay. At the first opportunity he again steered south-west for the land Pinzón had first sighted the previous day. Gradually the crews realised that what had seemed in the clear air of the previous sunset to be a distant land mass was really no such thing, but only a storm-cloud. When Columbus changed course again, back to their original one of due west, there were loud complaints from some of the seamen who did not want to accept that there was no land to the south-west.

Day after day they sailed on, always to the west. Because it was calm, Columbus could log only short distances each day—24 leagues, then 14, another 24, then 14 again. The weather was delightful, the air sweet and refreshing, lacking (according to Columbus) only the song of the nightingale. Once again, he likened the sea over which they were sailing to a wide river, bearing them onwards. They saw boobies and dark frigate birds. The latter, wrote Columbus, do not fly more than 20 miles from land; they live by attacking boobies which have just caught a fish and making them disgorge. Four black-and-white tropic birds flew to the ships, another sign of land nearby, thought Columbus. The mariners thought so too, and assuming that they were passing through a group of islands, wanted Columbus to go in search of them. To calm the men, he

64

The cathedral of Huelva, the home of Columbus's sister-in-law, in whose care he left his son Diego while petitioning at Court. *Courtesy Spanish National Tourist Office*

The monastery of La Rabida whose Prior, Juan Pérez, not only encouraged Columbus in his venture but played a key role in pleading his cause at the Spanish Court. *Courtesy Spanish National Tourist Office*

Navigational instruments from Henry VIII's flagship *Mary Rose*, laid down three years after the death of Columbus. They include a ship's compass, dividers, and a traverse board to record courses and distances run. Columbus would have had very similar instruments. *Courtesy Mary Rose Trust*

El Teide, the 12,162 feet high volcanic cone of Tenerife, a landmark for mariners for many miles. *Courtesy Spanish National Tourist Office*

continued to fake each day's figures, 24 leagues becoming 20, 14 becoming 13; a second 24 leagues was 21, and another 14 became merely 11. The last was on 30 September, which was Day Twenty-five.

During darkness on that day the pilots again became bewildered and disquieted by the curious behaviour of the compass. All the compasses misbehaved, not just one. At dawn the north-seeking needles pointed directly towards the Pole Star, Stella Maris, but as darkness came on it was seen that they strayed a whole point away. Penetrating vast and unknown regions of the globe, this was alarming. Columbus tried to quieten them by airing his own theory: the compass needles were always showing true north; it must be the Pole Star rotating above the Pole that was the cause of the discrepancy. Not all were fully convinced. But Columbus maintained that the compass did not lie, although he continued to do so.

On Day Twenty-six Columbus reckoned that they covered 25 leagues and told the crew only 20. He totted up the totals since leaving the last of the Canary islands, Hierro (or Ferro, according to the Portuguese). The true total distance since then, according to his private calculation, was 707 leagues; the total of the distances he had announced to the crew was 584 leagues. But these were not the only figures available. Peralonso Niño, the pilot of the *Santa Maria*, had of course been keeping his own (presumably honest) reckoning. He made the distance run west from Hierro as 578 leagues, close enough to Columbus's false figure of 584 to reinforce acceptance of it.

They were now into October and approaching the 28 days for which they had been stored and supplied. The crew, convinced from the various signs that islands must be near, although out of sight, again pressed Columbus to make a search for them; but this would have meant beating to windward and losing days. The trade winds were now blowing strongly westward and Columbus said it would be foolish to waste time in this manner at this precise moment. In the next five days they covered 39 leagues, then 63, followed by 46, then 57, then 40 leagues. Fast sailing indeed. The figures Columbus gave out to the crew were 30, 40, 46, 45, and 33. Many birds flew over and alighted on the ships; a boy in one of the caravels hit a booby with a stone. Many flying fish broke surface in fright from predators, and landed on the decks. Presumably, these and the birds were a source of food, by now bound to be extremely short.

Saturday, 6 October was Day Thirty-one. The full month was up since they had sailed from Gomera, provisioned for 28 days. Martin Alonso Pinzón, the very experienced captain of the *Pinta* caravel, that night suggested to Columbus an alteration of course to south-west by west, as according to the chart that Columbus had loaned him, that was now the course to reach the island of Cipangu. Columbus's stated reasons for refusing are not at all clear. They appear to imply a belief that the main island of Japan was quite small; they might easily miss it, and if so would have a much longer journey to reach the mainland of China beyond that. They kept on to the west, all jockeying for position to be the first to sight land. No doubt the *Santa Maria*'s mainmast overtopped those of the swifter caravels, but Pinzón's *Pinta*, the fastest of them all, sped on ahead.

At sunrise, a vivid flash and a dense cloud of smoke blossomed from the *Pinta*'s side. Many seconds later came the sharp thud of the gun, a bombard; and a standard went fluttering up to her masthead—the agreed signal that land had been sighted, that the Royal reward was claimed by Martin Alonso Pinzón.

Columbus's ruling had been that at both sunrise and sunset the ships should come together. This was because at those times the sea haze usually dispersed and visibility was at its maximum. And if the ships were close, the advantage would lie with the vessel having the highest lookout post, almost certainly the flagship.

It was now Sunday, 7 October. Day Thirty-two. But that evening, when the mists cleared away, no one could see the land the men of the *Pinta* thought they had glimpsed at daybreak. Wishful thinking, and a Royal reward, had once again transformed a dark cloud on the far horizon to the first outpost of the Indies.

However, Columbus took an important decision. At this time a great flock of birds passed over the little squadron, winging away to the south-west, as if seeking a roosting place or perhaps migrating. He knew from the years he had spent with the Portuguese that many of their island discoveries had been due to observing with attention the flight of birds. He now ordered the course to be altered to south-west, to follow in the track of the birds. And this was also just what Pinzón had been suggesting, from his reading of the chart. Columbus would not try out this course for no more than two days, initially. One hour before sunset the squadron turned away to the south-west.

To restrain the men's excitement, Columbus warned that any one who cried out 'Land! Land!' unnecessarily or lightly would forfeit the reward even if afterwards he should genuinely be the first to make the discovery. He defined this by laying down a period of three days' subsequent sailing to confirm the sighting. He repeated what he had always said, as a result of his cosmographical researches, that they would have to cover a distance of 750 leagues west of the Canaries before they could reasonably expect to reach land. In modern terms, perhaps 2,600 miles.

On Day Thirty-three the trade winds and the current marched together so that they sailed as if down 'the river of Seville'. Many birds were observed—terns, ducks, a booby—and they were all flying on the same course as the squadron, to the south-west. Next day, all through the night, they heard birds passing over them.

On 10 October it was Day Thirty-five. They logged 59 leagues, more than 200 miles in 24 hours, although Columbus admitted to only 44 leagues. Nevertheless, despite—or perhaps because of—this rapid progress, the men complained of the time the voyage was taking. For once, Columbus logged this complaint. He wrote that he told the men that protests were useless, he intended to go to the Indies, and would persevere until he found them.

By Friday, 11 October they had been at sea, sailing west, for 36 days with no sight of land. They were now going west-south-west in the roughest sea they had experienced so far. From the *Santa Maria* they saw petrels and fresh, green seaweed floating past the ship. Those in the caravel *Pinta* of Martin Alonso Pinzón saw a reed and a stick at first and later secured samples of another small stick and a piece of reed. The stick appeared to have been carved with a knife. From the caravel *Nina* other welcome signs were noted—including a small twig with roses on it. The tension evaporated and the men could breathe again.

Once again the *Pinta* jockeyed into the lead; once more the bombard thudded out its message and the success flag ran up to the masthead. This sighting was made by a seaman named Rodrigo de Triana. However, that night at ten o'clock, standing on the vantage point of the *Santa Maria*'s sterncastle, Columbus claimed to have seen a faint light in the darkness ahead. It was too dim to be quite certain, so he called on Pedro Gutiérrez, officer of the Royal household, to look out for it also. Gutiérrez confirmed the sighting. But the Royal inspector, Rodrigo Sanchez de Segovia, could see nothing. Columbus said that this was because he was standing in the wrong place.

Now a number of people were trying to make out the light, which waxed and waned like a small candle. Few thought this was evidence of land, but Columbus was certain. He ordered the singing of the *Salve*, and once the crew were all on deck and together, warned them to keep a good lookout from the forecastle. There would be a silk doublet on the spot for the first man to cry out 'Land!' (apart from the Royal reward in due course of a pension of 10,000 *maravedis* a year).

Two hours after midnight, land was sighted from the *Santa Maria* about two leagues distant. This was no storm cloud clinging to the horizon but cliffs pale in the moonlight, and a darker mass which must be trees.

They furled all canvas except the mainsail, bare without its bonnets, and lay idling in the darkness, waiting for daylight.

7
The Time of Triumph

Cautiously the fleet glided in towards the land, with due ritual of conquest. Flags were hoisted and long pennants streamed out in the wind. Gaily decorated shields—in English, 'pavesses'—were hung over the rails, partly ostentation, partly as protection against missiles.

The lookouts perched high in the tops or out on the yards reported a swell breaking on a reef which seemed to ring what was clearly an island, low-lying but green. For almost two leagues they coasted along its sheltered side, breathing the delicious scents of fertile land, before discovering a gap wide enough for the ships to sail through. Inside, they anchored off a shallowly shelving beach and prepared to put an armed party ashore.

Columbus donned his scarlet doublet; his officers also dressed in their best uniforms, and fastened on their swords, the others carrying short pikes or crossbows. As Columbus stepped out of the boat into the warm, shallow water, he bore the Royal standard up the beach. Behind him came the two caravel captains, Martin Alonso Pinzón of the *Pinta* and Vicente Yáñez Pinzón of the *Nina*. Both the Pinzón brothers carried green-cross banners emblazoned with the crown and the letters F and Y, for the royal pair Ferdinand and Ysabela (as Spaniards spelt her name). And behind them the two crown officials, Rodrigo Escobedo and Rodrigo Sanchez de Segovia, to witness the event.

After formally taking possession of the island in the name of his sponsors, the King and Queen of Spain, Columbus said a prayer:

> O Lord, Almighty and Everlasting God, by Thy holy Word Thou hast created the heaven, and the earth, and the sea; blessed and glorified be Thy Name, and praised be Thy Majesty, Which hath deigned to use us, Thy humble servants, that Thy holy Name may be known and proclaimed in this second part of the earth.

From that moment on, he truly was all the titles he had claimed and striven for: Grand Admiral of the Ocean, Viceroy of this island and Governor of it, too. So he named it San Salvador, Holy Saviour. His new subjects began to come out of the trees—young men and women, well built and handsome, with fine eyes and broad brows, neither white nor yet black but something in between, like the native inhabitants of the Canary Islands, the Guanches. And they were all stark naked, both the men and the women.

This was not the golden-roofed civilisation he had expected to meet on the mainland of Japan. On the contrary, this was a most primitive culture. They had no iron. Their spears were made of cane, sharpened to a point or tipped with bone. When he showed them a sword, they did not know what it was; and taking it by the sharp edge, cut themselves. A few, though, had wound scars on their bodies, and as far as Columbus could make out, these had been inflicted by the inhabitants of a nearby island, probably during a slave raid. Some had ornaments of gold, he was quick to note, and if he understood them aright, the source of the gold lay over the sea to the south-west.

They seemed a very gentle people, delighted with the small gifts of European goods which Columbus gave them, particularly the tiny brass bells which falconers tied to the legs of their hunting birds. They were very friendly and anxious to exchange what they had, such as spears or balls of cotton, for European products.

Columbus particularly logged the cotton, as a trade item of possible value to the Spanish crown, but excused himself from trying to find out how much of it San Salvador produced by writing that he was in haste to hurry on and discover the 'island of Cipangu', the mainland of Japan, whence, he suspected, the slave raiders came to prey on the peaceful people of Guanahani, as the natives themselves called this island. He thought they would make 'good servants', being very intelligent, quick to repeat words spoken to them in Spanish and, as they seemed to him to have no religion, might easily become Christians. There was no animal life there, except parrots, he noted.

At dawn on Sunday, 14 October, he ordered a boat expedition round the island, to explore it further, and saw a few villages whose inhabitants ran down the beaches bringing food and water and other gifts to the Spaniards and their Italian Admiral. Columbus captured seven of them, with the intention of teaching them Spanish and taking them back to Spain as living specimens of the nature of his conquest. It would be clear to all back home that they were 'very unskilled in arms' and, as Columbus noted, would be evidence of the fact that the entire population of San Salvador could, with 50 men, be subjugated and made to do whatever the Spanish Crown wished. There were groves of 'the loveliest trees I have seen', he recorded.

Columbus's log of this voyage has long been lost, as has a 'book' he wrote. But various historians had the use of them and based their accounts on this material, sometimes quoting verbatim, at other times merely summarising. A few had the advantage of knowing Columbus personally.

Columbus takes possession of an island and is greeted by natives bringing gifts more elaborate than most of them actually were. Note the cross being erected on the headland, as symbol of Spanish conquest. Engraving by Theodore de Bry, published in *Americae*, pars IV, Frankfurt, 1594. *Courtesy National Maritime Museum*

The most distinguished was Bishop Bartholomé Las Casas, who wrote his *Historia de las Indias* (History of the Indies) between 1527 and 1561, with original manuscripts before him—and in the knowledge that the gentle, generous natives of Guanahani had been exterminated.

> I have no doubt that if the Admiral had believed that such dreadful results would follow and had known as much about the primary and secondary effects of natural and divine law as he knew about cosmography and other human learning, he would never have introduced or initiated a practice which was to lead to such terrible harm. For no one can deny that he was a good and Christian man.
>
> It would be well to point out two things: first, the natural willingness and predisposition of these people to receive our holy faith and their readiness to adopt Christianity and moral virtues, if treated with love, charity and kindness; how profitable this would have been to

God; and secondly, how far the Admiral was from the punctual observation of divine and natural law, and how little he understood the sovereigns' obligations and his own to the natives, according to this law, since he could so lightly say that they might take all the Indians who were the natural inhabitants of these lands to Castile, or hold them captive on their own island . . .

This was very far from the purpose of God and His Church, to which this voyage and the discovery of all this world and everything in and about it should have been subordinated, and by which it should have been directed.

Columbus set sail again that Sunday evening of 14 October, 1492, and saw so many islands on the horizon that he did not know which one to investigate first. The seven natives he had kidnapped from San Salvador told him by signs that there were so many it was impossible to count them. They recited more than one hundred names. Columbus chose what

A fanciful portrayal of Columbus among the islands of the Indies. From a woodcut, Basle, 1494. *Courtesy of the Trustees of the British Museum*

71

seemed to be the largest and headed for that. This was embarrassing. Theoretically, he should take formal possession of every single island in the name of his sponsors, Ferdinand and Isabella, but it would be a slow process, cautiously coasting along in shallow water among unknown reefs, forced to lie-to during the hours of darkness. His final choice was determined by what he understood the captive natives to say about the likelihood of finding gold (although he suspected that they might be lying, in the hope of escaping from captivity).

He named the island Santa Maria de la Concepción, and two natives from San Salvador did indeed escape when a dugout canoe came alongside the caravel *Nina*. One Salvadorean jumped into it and another dived overboard and swam to the canoe as it made off, so fast that it could not be overtaken.

Then another small canoe, with one man in it, approached the *Nina*, apparently wanting to trade a ball of cotton but now fearful and unwilling to come on board. Seamen from the caravel jumped down, seized him and bundled him aboard the Spanish vessel. Columbus, who had been standing on the forecastle, ordered the native to be brought to him. In a gesture of friendship he gave the man a red cap as a present, together with some green glass beads for his arm and two hawk's bells to put in his ears. The canoe was restored to him, and the man paddled it ashore and could be seen on the beach, surrounded by a large crowd.

Columbus hoped that this would create a good impression to offset that of the forcible kidnapping of the seven men from San Salvador, as he noted in the log:

> I was anxious that they should think well of us so that they may not be unfriendly when your Majesties send a second expedition here. All I gave him was worth less than four maravedis.

As a *maravedi* was worth perhaps less than the old English farthing, this entry was bound to impress the businessmen and the Royal accountants back in Spain, as well as the diplomats.

The natives, however, were pathetically eager for souvenirs of any sort from these wonderful strangers. They seemed to think that they had come from the sky. Columbus saw some of the ship's boys exchanging small sherds of broken crockery or glass for native spears.

Throughout the second half of October they sailed from island to island. One he named for King Ferdinand and another for Queen Isabella. The latter was at first only a native tale, a city—or an island, he could not be sure which—called Samoet where, the natives said, there was much gold. It was absolutely essential that they discover a goldmine or at least a rich trading city. Otherwise, their venture would have failed.

Navigating among these islands proved to be easier than expected, for the water was extraordinarily clear. The bottom appeared patchy, with dark areas of rock and stretches of clean sand. From the deck, and better still from the mastheads, the nature of the terrain could be clearly seen; except in very deep water. And there Columbus hesitated to anchor for fear of getting foul; so far from base, he could not afford to lose anchors.

He was surprised to note how different the fish were from those he was accustomed to: different in shape, sometimes startlingly so, and varied in colour—bright blues, vivid yellows, rich reds flickered among the submerged reefs in unbelievable splendour. The sight gave them all immense pleasure.

Ashore, although the islands were marvellously fertile and of great beauty, they saw few animals—many birds, including multi-coloured parrots, some lizards, a snake or two. The native villages consisted of perhaps a dozen huts. But there were a myriad flowers and delicious scents. In this warm, temperate paradise, the natives felt no need to wear clothes, although some of the women wore a small piece of cotton in front to hide their feminine parts. What the natives lacked in the way of dress they made up for by painting their bodies in vivid hues—white, red, black. Their huts were clean inside, with beds and blankets made like cotton nets, called *hamaca*. (Adopted by European seamen, they came to be called hammocks.) The natives used fires to boil certain roots for food and to burn 'perfumed herbs' for which their word was *caoba*. They sniffed them through Y-shaped tubes they called *tabaca*. The cotton did not have to be cultivated, it grew wild, unlike the fields of roots, beans and grain. The only four-footed animals the Spaniards saw were dogs which did not bark. Judging by how near to the shore the trees, grasses and plants grew,

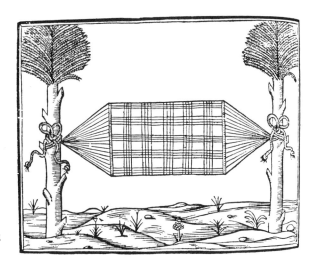

The *hamaca* of the natives of the Caribbean, later adopted by European seamen. From a book published in Spain, 1547.

Columbus assumed that there were no really destructive storms to be expected in these regions, unlike the mountainous waves which in winter sweep European coastlines.

On 19 October the fleet had split in order to widen the search to locate the fabulous isle of Samoet where there was supposed to be a king who wore much gold on his person. The island was found that day and Columbus determined to locate the king and get the gold off him.

Even more exciting vistas loomed ahead, for the captured natives on board the ships were understood to say that there were two great islands not far away, the nearest being called Colba, the other Bohio. At Colba, they indicated, were many large ships and seamen. Columbus concluded that this must be Cipangu.

According to Marco Polo, Japan was a vast island, 1,500 miles from the mainland of what we called Asia, whose inhabitants had 'white skins and beautiful manners'; they mined gold in 'huge quantities'. The supreme ruler had a palace roofed not with lead but with gold and the floors of the bedrooms were laid with gold two fingers thick. And there were large, beautiful pink pearls in vast numbers. Kublai Khan, attracted by these riches, had in 1281 mounted an immense seaborne invasion which was overwhelmed by a great storm, which the Japanese ever after called the 'Divine Wind', the *Kamikaze*.

Tempting though this immediate prospect was, Columbus recorded that he was still determined to press on to the rich city of Quinsay in China, personally to deliver the Royal letters of credit to the Great Khan and request his answer.

Marco Polo had never been to Japan but he had spent many years in China and in his book he had been explicit about the great city of Kinsai on its tidal river, threaded by canals. That city, he wrote, was 100 miles across, possessed 12,000 stone bridges, besides many wooden ones, had 1,600,000 houses, many grand palaces and 3,000 hot baths, but only one Christian church. The annual revenue was 14,700,000 pieces of gold.

According to the globes and painted maps of the world which Columbus had seen during his travels and enquiries, they must now be very near Cipangu, and this agreed with what the native prisoners said: that in their log boats, which had no sails but had to be paddled, Colba was only a day and a half's journey away. According to them, the ships of the Great Khan came to the large island they called Colba from the mainland, which was ten days' journey farther on.

Sailing south-south-west, on 28 October the expedition reached Colba, which proved to be a very high island, like Sicily, and well wooded; indeed, on many days or nights it rained, so they were in no danger of dying of thirst. There was a number of sizeable rivers, which they could enter and sail upstream for a bombard's shot or more.

Native hut similar to those found by Columbus at the anchorage he named Puerto de Mares. From a book published in Spain, 1547.

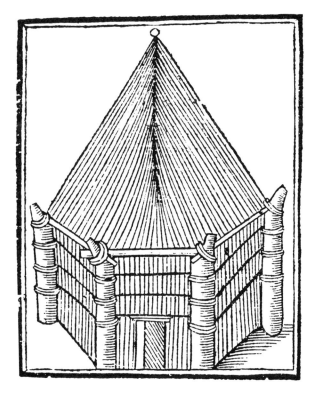

The widest and best, because it was flanked by a rocky hill ideal as the base for a fortress covering the entrance, Columbus named Rio de Mares and the anchorage Puerto de Mares. He noted that the native houses here were of the same general type they had seen before, but larger, more elaborate, better, which he took for a sign that they were near civilisation. The dwellings were like enormous Moorish tents, with very steep-pitched roofs made of palm leaves, calculated to decant heavy tropical rainstorms. There were doorways but no doors, allowing adequate ventilation.

The three San Salvadorean natives who were prisoners in the *Pinta* told Pinzón that 'Colba' was not the name of the country but of a city inland from this coast; at least, that is what he thought they were trying to tell him. So Columbus sent off an embassy consisting of two of the San Salvadorean natives and two of his own men—Rodrigo de Jérez from Ayamonte and Luis de Torres, the interpreter. They were to ask to speak to the King and explain that they were representing the Catholic Sovereigns of Castile.

Columbus was now sure that these estuaries represented part of the mainland of Cathay and that his ships were now 300 miles, more or less, from Zayto and Quinsay where the real riches of the Indies were to be found. What made him certain was partly the scend or driving impulse of the sea, which was quite different on this coast from what it had been before, and also the distance run from Hierro, the last of the Canaries group—1,142 leagues or 3,426 miles. He decided that this was a convenient time and place to overhaul the ships, always a ticklish proceeding.

He ordered the *Nina* in first for cleaning, while the *Pinta* and *Santa Maria* remained afloat, armed and manned. The procedure was to beach the vessel at high water, then by tying ropes to the masts literally to haul her over on one side. The exposed side would then be scraped clean of seagrowth—weed, barnacles and so on—and then 'paid' with hot pitch to discourage any timber-hungry marine organisms. Then the other side would be similarly treated. If time allowed, all stores would have been removed, the hold and decks fumigated with smoke, and the caulking renewed where necessary. While this was going on, the vessel and her crew would be vulnerable and helpless, completely exposed to attack by hostile natives or a raging sea. Columbus complacently observed that the natives, so far from being hostile, were notably timid, and that he had not once on the voyage so far met with any severe gales.

After the *Nina* had been cleaned and then re-stored and re-floated, he sent the *Pinta* in to be overhauled and cleaned, and when she was once more afloat, finally beached the *Santa Maria* while the two caravels kept guard. This was another advantage of using only small vessels for such voyages of exploration. A large carrack would have been two huge and heavy for the available manpower and material resources.

When the ships were ready to voyage farther, Columbus detained on board a dozen men, women and children from the local tribe—'in a peaceful way, without noise or trouble'—and then set off to the south-east for the land called by the natives Bohio or Babeque. At the last moment the head of one of the newly kidnapped families paddled out in a canoe and pleaded to be taken aboard also, so as not to be separated from his wife and children. Columbus was delighted to have, for once, an eager passenger. Some of the San Salvadoreans had already attempted to escape, and several had succeeded.

They were now trying to sail back more or less into wind, which was a slow and frustrating process. At night they had to stand off from the land for fear of hidden reefs or shallows. The islands they saw were very high but with no sign of snow on their peaks (unlike Tenerife), set in a very deep sea; and all so beautiful that Columbus ran out of words to describe them; each vista seemed more splendid than the last. He believed them to be the very same isles as were depicted on many world maps of the Indies and that they must therefore be rich in jewels and spices. When he found suitable harbours, he erected a wooden cross both to mark the entrance and also to proclaim that he had taken possession of this fresh part of his new kingdom on behalf of the Sovereigns of Spain.

In mid-November he decided to explore farther, using the ships' boats, presumably under sail, and when he returned to the *Santa Maria* found that his captive Indians were skin-diving for conches. These made good souvenirs and ornaments but Columbus thought that their diving time would be better spent in picking pearl-oysters off the bottom. Many oysters were brought up, but there were no pearls in them. However, from the boats a number of potential harbours were surveyed.

Some members of the fleet may have become impatient with the tame work of survey, vital though it would be to an imperial power, and perhaps Columbus's continually expressed belief that gold in fabulous quantities was just waiting over the horizon to be found, may have persuaded others. Anyway, on 21 November Martin Alonso Pinzón sailed off on his own in the *Pinta*, the fastest vessel of the three, without consulting the Admiral, who made bitter complaint. His 'fleet' was now reduced to two vessels.

It was slowly becoming clear that 'Babeque', where Pinzón had gone, and 'Bohio', were two separate places. The native prisoners showed fear at the thought of landing on Bohio, a large and lofty island, and Columbus understood them to say that it was the home of the Caniba, Canima, Caribs or Canibales, dog-faced people with only one eye who ate human flesh. Always the optimist, he took this for evidence that Bohio was in the domain of the Great Khan of Cathay, and it was the wrath of the Great Khan, not the mythical Canibales, whom they really feared.

Off the coast of Bohio, giving shelter to the mouths of its natural harbours, lay a small isle which Columbus named Isla de la Tortuga, Tortoise Island. The fish they netted now were known to them from their own Spanish coasts—unlike the exotic specimens which inhabited the reefs of the coral islands. The landscape also seemed similar to their homeland. Some of the native girls were as white as a maiden from Castile. For all these reasons Columbus on Sunday, 9 December, gave Bohio its new name of La Isla Española, the Spanish Island. He was still unaware how woefully he misunderstood what his native captives said. 'Bohio' was not their name for the island, it was their word for a house.

Seashell from the Caribbean.
Courtesy Bahamas Tourist Office

Nevertheless, he was overwhelmed by the beauty of this 'enchanted land' and the contrast with the fever coast of Guinea and its poisonous rivers; the sweet and temperate climate here, the clear, clean water of both seas and rivers. Thus far, he claimed, in all three ships there had been only one case of sickness since leaving home, and this exception was an old man in pain from kidney stones, from which he had suffered all his life. Apart from him, no one had been laid up with illness, no one had even complained of a headache.

So enthusiastic did Columbus become that he later advised the Spanish Sovereigns not to allow any foreigners to set foot there or trade, but to keep his discovery the sole preserve of Catholic Christians, since the whole idea of his enterprise was for the glory of God. 'No one should come here who is not a good Christian.'

Initially, the Spaniards had trouble convincing the natives of their good intent. Three of the explorers surprised a group of locals who, without the hindrance of clothes, outran them into the dense woods. All they could catch was a girl, naked except for a flat piece of gold hanging from her nose. When brought before the Admiral, she was given a few trinkets and little bells and released unharmed, as a token of Spanish goodwill. The native prisoners already aboard could not tell her the truth because they did not know; though they understood that they would be released as soon as the explorers found gold; in fact Columbus always intended to bring them back to Castile as proof of his triumph and as potential interpreters to later expeditions, which would conquer and occupy.

On hearing yet another story that the gold they sought was still farther east, upwind, they sailed off and tried to make headway in that direction, beating about between Tortoise Island and Spanish Island. They had arrived with the trade winds; to go against them was slow work and often meant keeping closer in to shore than was safe. In rough seas they sighted a native canoe with one man in it and rescued him. Then they went back to their previous anchorage on Española, where the rescued man gave such a good account of them that the Spaniards were visited by a chief and his entourage whom Columbus wined and dined at an eating table set up under the forecastle of the *Santa Maria*. When they left, Columbus ordered a gun salute fired, and the bombards thundered and thudded out their respect to the chief who was carried off up the beach on a litter, accompanied by 200 of his followers.

They sailed again after midnight on 19 December, because that was the time when light breezes blew off the land towards the east, whereas the daytime winds were foul for them on an eastward course. New headlands came into view and a blue mountain in the distance, which Columbus, thinking it lay in the land of the ferocious Caribs, named Monte Caribata. On 20 December, before nightfall, they were towed in among the reefs by

The more common type of
native hut, less grand than those
at Puerto de Mares. From a book
published in Spain, 1547.

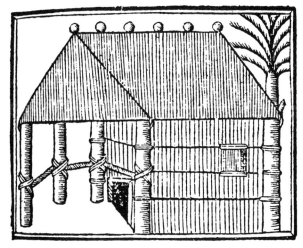

their boats to a great inlet forming an immense and well-screened harbour.
As it was the feast day of Saint Thomas Columbus called it Puerto de la Mar
Santo Tomás. In his report, he said that although he had sailed the seas for
23 years, almost continually, had seen all of the West and all of the East,
and had even been to Guinea (which was in the Portuguese sphere of
exploration), he had never seen such harbours as there were in these
lands, and this one surpassed them all.

Better still, natives came down to the shore in their thousands and put
out to the ships in canoes or, if they were without transport, just swam
out. They brought gifts of all kinds: calabashes of water, food, cotton,
parrots, gold—and they seemed to value the gold as much or as little as the
calabashes full of water. Noticing that the Spaniards appreciated gold,
they added that there was more of it a few miles farther along the coast to
the east, in the land of the chief Guacanagari. This chief requested a visit
and his envoys presented Columbus with a belt which had a golden mask
on it instead of a pouch.

The Admiral sent off a reconnaissance mission, using the boats since
there was no wind, in order to survey the reefs which outcropped all along
this coast between St Thomas Harbour and Guacanagari's village. His idea
was to use the offshore winds which sprang up during the night to get the
ships eastward, and this would mean hugging a dangerous coast in the
dark. It was vital to survey their course in advance. The lure eastward, as
ever, was the rumour of a gold source in that direction.

Reading between the lines of Columbus's report, the risk was accepted
not merely out of greed for gold but out of a well-being stemming from the
extraordinary friendliness of the local natives, including the women.
Here, as everywhere, they went naked without self-consciousness, and

were extremely well-formed and of a colour almost as pale as that of the Europeans; and, for once, were not guarded or restrained by their men. No doubt the eagerness of the European seamen proved flattering as well as exciting, especially as they seemed to appear to the natives as gods from another world.

When the *Santa Maria* sailed again, on 24 December, in order to catch the night wind blowing easterly offshore, and tacked out to sea to round the great headland that lay along their route, Columbus wrote that he had not slept for two days and a night, but took the first watch and then went to his bed at 11 o'clock that evening. Next day would be Christmas Day.

If he dreamed, they must have been golden dreams. The natives had told him (he thought) that the source of the gold was farther east, in a land called Cibao. Certainly (he thought) that could only mean Cipangu, the civilised land where the houses had roofs of gold. The great dream, the dream of years, was about to come true; tomorrow, on Christmas Day.

The way out to open sea beyond the reefs ringing the great headland of Monte Caribata had been hard work, and tricky. The offshore wind died away. In dim moonlight the remaining caravel, the *Nina*, was just visible ahead. The two European vessels were drifting rather than sailing, their canvas slack, carried by the current and onshore swell. No ship's boy should have been given the tiller, but the helmsman was tired; he pointed out a star to a drowsy boy, gave him the heavy tiller, and told him to keep the star where it was now, to steer on that. Then he closed his eyes for a moment.

Columbus was to write that he had forbidden such delegation of so important a duty to a ship's boy, a duty in any case likely to be beyond his strength. And he maintained that anyone could have heard the sinister warning roar of the swell lifting lazily over the barely submerged reefs a few hundred yards away. Anyway, it was the master's watch, the entire responsibility of Juan de la Cosa, the Basque, who was also the owner of the *Santa Maria* and had the greatest investment in the safety of the ship. No matter. The revelry of the previous days had taken its toll.

The ship's boy, hand obediently on the heavy tiller, was the first to feel the rudder scrape the reef and hear the hollow sound it made. He screamed in panic.

Columbus reached the deck before Juan de la Cosa, who was officially on watch. The Admiral gave immediate order for de la Cosa and some of the seamen to man the ship's boat, towing astern, to put an anchor in it and take that anchor out to seaward, so that by hauling in on it, they might pull the flagship off the reef.

The kedge party, led by the master, pulled the boat up to the *Santa Maria* and got into it. But not to kedge off. They left their stricken ship and rowed for the safety of the *Nina*, visible about half a league away.

80

The interor of Tenerife, a difficult country to conquer against the stiff resistance put up by the native Guanches, as the Spaniards found. *Courtesy Spanish National Tourist Office*

A beach on the island of Gomera, with its grey volcanic sand. *Courtesy Spanish National Tourist Office*

The modern port of San Sebastian, Gomera. *Courtesy Spanish National Tourist Office*

Marco Polo sets out from Venice: a picture dating from about 1400, showing some believable ships of the period. *Courtesy Bodleian Library, Oxford*

The current slowly swung the *Santa Maria* round, so that she lay broadside to the reef, virtually helpless. The timbers trembled and protested. Then they were stove and water burst into the hull. The tide was falling and the swell roared, sucking back from the fangs of coral which held her. More planks parted at their seams and the sea flooded in until the hold was full. His flagship pinned and broken beneath him, Columbus ordered the masts cut away in a last effort to lighten her, the ultimate order of despair.

8
Two Bids for Immortality

The flagship lay almost broadside to the reef, the contents of the hold and lower deck afloat, banging and grumbling beneath their feet as the casks stirred sluggishly with the sea washing about inside the *Santa Maria*. The tide fell still farther and the now mastless hulk was clearly doomed. The captain of the *Nina*, Vicente Yáñez Pinzón of Palos, sent his own boat over to help, at the same time refusing refuge to Juan de la Cosa, owner and master of the *Santa Maria*, whose plain duty was to stand by the wrecked flagship and help to get her off. Why the man had panicked cannot now be known; possibly because, as Columbus wrote, he had been on watch at the time of the accident and could therefore be held directly responsible.

Columbus sent one boat ashore with Diego de Harana, the little fleet's provost marshal, and Pedro Gutiérrez, officer of the royal household, to request help from the friendly local chief, Guacanagari. The Admiral himself went over to the *Nina*, because from now onward this must be his ship. Indeed, it was the only ship he had, as Martin Alonso Pinzón had deserted him in the *Pinta* in order to discover the gold of Babeque.

When the chief Guacanagari heard that Columbus had lost his ship on a reef a league and a half offshore, he seemed very sad. Then he acted. He sent all his people in their canoes out to the wreck and with their aid the decks were cleared and everything brought ashore, to be stored in three native houses emptied for that purpose, and guarded by some of his men.

Columbus was grateful, writing to assure his Sovereigns that such kindness as he had received would never have been met with in Castile. The natives were, he said, affectionate and without greed, and so amenable that there could be no better anywhere in the world. 'They love their neighbours as themselves, they are always gentle and smiling.' Their chief, or *cacique*, kept a kingly state 'yet with a certain kind of modesty that is a pleasure to behold'.

On 26 December, the *cacique* himself came out to Columbus who had now installed himself as Admiral in the *Nina*, and offered any further help the Europeans might stand in need of. A large canoe from another island arrived, bringing sheets of gold as bartering objects for the bells which the natives coveted above all other European goods. Noting the Admiral's reaction to the sight of this gold, Guacanagari promised him much more,

82

which would be brought from Cibao, the place that had the most. Columbus still assumed that Cibao was merely the native pronunciation of Cipangu.

Before going ashore the *cacique* invited the Admiral to a feast of sweet potatoes and yucca and gave him native artefacts as gifts: they included masks made partly out of gold. He complained of the Carib Canibales who raided his people in order to eat them. Columbus took the opportunity to show him the use of European weapons. The pikes were paralleled by the bone-tipped cane spears of the natives; the deadliness of sword and dagger was clear enough, although a demonstration of their use both as offensive and defensive weapons was required. But the ordnance—the bombards and swivel-guns—was a different matter. They were simply tubes with no obvious purpose.

Columbus decided to spend a little powder and shot, using the hull of

A somewhat exaggerated impression of the riches of the Caribbean, in this illustration of natives bringing treasures for barter. Engraving by Theodore de Bry, published in *Americae*, pars IV, Frankfurt, 1594. *Courtesy National Maritime Museum*

the sunken *Santa Maria* as a target. A gunner applied the match to a touch-hole, and at the sound of the detonation the natives 'fell down like dead men' with fright. The sight of the ball passing right through both sides of the *Santa Maria* and falling into the water on the far side both 'horrified and amazed' the chief. The castling at least of the *nao* was probably no stouter than any modern garden shed, but in this place, to these people, the power of penetration demonstrated by the weapon was awe-inspiring.

The Admiral then offered the use of his men and their weapons as defence against the Caribs. He had already decided to make the best he could out of his apparent misfortune. Perhaps God had ordained that he should create the first Christian settlement here by wrecking his ship. He had too many men for the *Nina* to take, as well as the now surplus armament salvaged from the wreck. A fort could be constructed from her timbers and defended by her guns. There would be no shortage of volunteers to man it. The sight of natives continually bringing in gold convinced many that they had only to wait and they would become rich.

His mind rapidly arranged the details. Thirty-six men were chosen, among them carpenters, caulkers, a doctor, a tailor and so on; and over them three responsible officers, Diego de Harana of Cordova, the provost marshal, Pedro Gutiérrez, officer of the royal household, and Rodrigo de Escobedo, secretary. They were fully supplied with arms, and with provisions, and were left the flagship's longboat. They were to maintain good relations with the natives, to learn their language and to gather information. So, when Columbus returned, he would have available to him a useful staff for 'the conquest and occupation of the country'. Indeed, the misfortune to the *Santa Maria* might well have been the result of divine intervention.

This rapid change of mood and the speed and enthusiasm with which Columbus constructed an alternative plan were a necessary part of his character; the same as that which convinced him that Japan and China were only a few days' sail distant, and that unimaginable riches must be almost within his grasp. No pessimist could have even dreamt of doing what he had done, let alone plan it, plead for it, and actually carry it out. Optimism founded upon belief was the prime qualification for the task—plus the ability to convince others.

On Friday, 4 January of the new year, 1493, Columbus, Admiral of one ship, raised sail and went away to the north-west, leaving behind him the Christian settlement he had founded. He had named it Puerto de la Navidad, Christmas Harbour, for the season at which it was constructed out of the wreckage of the flag *nao*. As the caravel and its twenty-six men picked its way between the reefs and shoals which stretched for six leagues along the coast before an exit could be made to open sea, Columbus noted the leading 'marks' which would allow a second expedition to find the settlement. The initial point was a high mountain, shaped like a bell tent, which he named Monte Christi. But about his return course to Spain he was much less forthcoming, presumably wishing to retain as a personal secret the means of a speedy return before favourable winds.

For some reason which he did not explain, Columbus at first turned eastwards and met the predictable unfavourable winds; and shortly after, a caulker on lookout duty in the main top sighted the *Pinta* sailing rapidly towards them with the prevailing westerly. Her captain, Martin Alonso Pinzón, came on board the *Nina* and, according to the Admiral, gave him 'invented excuses and false arguments' to explain why he had left the fleet. Columbus labelled him 'dishonest' and complained of the 'liberties' he had taken during the voyage, but pretended to believe what Pinzón said because the success of the expedition still depended on keeping harmony with the Pinzón family and their followers, who formed the majority of the officers and crews of the two caravels.

In his log Columbus reported that the truth of the matter was that some of the captive Indians kept aboard the *Pinta* had told Pinzón that there was much gold on the isle of Babeque; but when the Spaniard had found this to be untrue he had followed yet another native story and returned to Bohio, now Española, and in 20 days had got no farther than fifteen leagues east of where the Admiral had lost his flagship. However, he also had found there natives willing to trade gold for trash. Half of the gold he had shared out among his crew, keeping the other half for himself (although, to Columbus, he denied it).

Still Columbus did not leave for Spain. Both caravels were leaking more than was normal and had to be beached for re-caulking; and the opportunity was taken to fill the water casks and collect a store of sweet potatoes and buy from the local natives strong peppers called *axi* (known today as chillies or paprikas). During this time there was a small skirmish with a group of natives much fiercer than usual, who blackened their faces with soot (instead of using colours) and wore their hair long and tied at the back like the women of Castile. There were about 55 of them and only seven Spaniards from a boat party, but European weapons were superior and the natives retired with two men wounded—one with an arrow in the chest and another with a swordcut in his rear. Columbus welcomed this small affray as a useful lesson to the locals, both friendly and unfriendly. Their discarded bows, he said, were of yew and 'almost as stout as those of the French and English'.

The bay where this happened he named the Golfo de las Flechas, and a nearby river which he had explored by boat and in which he found grains of gold he called Rio del Oro. The source could not be more than twenty leagues inland, he thought. Having once seen the wonder of a gold mine on the Portuguese-held coast of Guinea, he had no difficulty in visualising some nearby place where gold could be had from the ground with little toil.

On 16 January, 1493, the two caravels left the Gulf of the Arrows and set course for Castile. Columbus was now in a bad temper, inwardly raging at the Pinzón family and their followers as malcontents who had impeded his successful voyage, and thinking bitterly back to all the lost years he had been forced to waste while pleading his case through the courts of kings. The sceptics, the scholars, the old cosmographers with their underlying doubts and their sharp questions, had cost him fully six years' delay in Spain alone. The exploitation of the Indies by Spain had been set back by that amount of time. How much would that be in terms of cash? he argued to himself. A hundred millions?

Mentally, he may have been rehearsing all the arguments he might logically expect to meet on his return to court. Few men relish being shown to be mistaken, and scholars least of all. He had claimed to be able to find the way to Cipangu and Cathay, and where was the evidence? Gold? A few native trinkets only. Where were the great civilisations of the East, the cities a hundred miles across, ruled by great kings—to whom he was to have delivered his Royal letters of credit? Nowhere, for he was bringing the letters back. What had he discovered? A race of gentle, primitive tribesmen whose largest 'town' consisted of a few hundred huts, and another race of more savage people. And some beautiful scenery and a few splendid anchorages. And yet he *had* discovered it; all had been unknown until he had ventured there. His mind seethed, meeting foreseen objections.

By 9 February, having favourable winds and fast sailing, the other navigators put them close to the Azores. Vicente Yáñez Pinzón, captain of the *Nina*, thought their position to be south of Flores and east of Madeira. Bartholomé Roldán, one of the convicted criminals allowed to join the venture as an alternative sentence, and beginning to take an interest in the fascinating problems of finding a position with inadequate instruments from a pitching, rolling deck, put Fayal and Porto Santo in the north-east arc from where they were. But Columbus, who had spent part of his life on Porto Santo, judging mainly by the weed he had noted on the outward passage, thought the two caravels were still 150 leagues short of the Azores; even so, that made them halfway home.

The winds, increasing in strength, began to create an uncomfortable sea for the two low, leaky craft. On 14 February, nearly a month out from the Gulf of the Arrows, they had to run with the wind astern, more to the north than they wished, especially the *Pinta* which, although a fast sailer, was not as weatherly as the *Nina*. The course for Spain being north-east, Columbus was able to keep more nearly to it and soon lost sight of the

Pinta's light when darkness came. At daybreak, from the *Nina* there was no sign of the *Pinta*, and from the *Pinta* no sign of the *Nina*. The crews of each vessel assumed that the other had been overwhelmed and sunk. They were not far off it.

On the *Nina* the devout Catholics, led by Columbus, prayed to the Lord to help them through. As well as working in relays at the monotonous task of pumping water out faster than it could flow in, they made vows, promising to perform various services to God if He consented to save them. Because these vows could be expensive as well as onerous, they drew lots to decide who should perform them, using marked beans drawn from a cap. The first task agreed was a pilgrimage to Santa Maria de Guadelupe in the Spanish province of Estremadura. Columbus drew the marked bean. The next was a pilgrimage to Santa Maria de Loreto in the Papal States of Italy. A poor seaman, Pedro de Villa, drew that one, and the Admiral promised to pay his travelling expenses. Still the wind shrieked through the rigging and roared at the single mainsail they carried. So they drew a third time, for a man to keep a night-long vigil in Santa Clara de Moguer, not far from their homes in Spain. Columbus drew that one. The seas continued to batter at the stern of the caravel, spray sweeping the deck and the planks awash with water as she rolled. Ominously, the storm was increasing in intensity. Their peril was extreme.

They all prayed to the Virgin Mary. At the first church dedicated to the Virgin which they came to—if they were allowed to reach it—they would walk barefoot in their shirts to offer a prayer of gratitude.

The motion of the vessel was very awkward, and pumping out the water from the leaking hull was not merely ineffective but actually counter-productive. The caravel, with most of her provisions consumed, was riding higher in the waves than she had been a month ago. Someone conceived the idea which saved her—to fill the empty water casks and food barrels with seawater and then replace them low down in the hold as liquid ballast.

The Admiral later told his son, Fernando Colón, that what oppressed him during this time was not so much the thought of death as the realisation that, at the very moment when he had demonstrably proved all his opponents wrong, he would have perished without glory because no one would know what he had done.

A lesser factor was that he would also have been responsible for the deaths of those who had sailed with him, not very willingly and whom he had often forced to carry on with the voyage in spite of their reluctance. Now finding themselves in terrible danger, they were openly cursing Columbus.

It was less hard to feel sorrow for his two sons, whom he had placed as

87

students in Cordova: they would be left without support in Spain, a land foreign to them, and surrounded by foreigners. Worse, they might think their father a failure, unaware that he had in fact performed the task which he had promised the Sovereigns and the Church to attempt. Indeed, it might be said that he had gained a victory, which Spain could turn to her advantage if only the two Sovereigns knew of it. Even if the *Nina* now sank, and he with her, there must be some way of passing on the message.

The Admiral's solution was to write on parchment a brief account of his discoveries, with a description and details of how to reach them, not forgetting the vital point that he had already taken possession of those lands in the names of Ferdinand and Isabella. He folded the parchment, sealed it and added a note that the man who delivered it unopened to the royal pair should receive a thousand ducats for his trouble. Then the parchment was wrapped in cloth and enclosed in a coating of wax to keep it dry, and the whole package put into a cask which was thrown overboard somewhat to the west of the Azores.

The likelihood of it being found seemed remote. Columbus therefore prepared another message, made it waterproof in the same way, enclosed it in another cask and had that cask placed at the highest point of the bow, so that it would burst free only if the ship sank, on the same principle as the modern ship's liferaft.

A surviving letter of Columbus, written on this return voyage, expresses what must have been in these messages abandoned to the storm, showing what, at the moment of his triumph, he felt he had achieved. What the natives called *Colba* and thought to be a large island could be none other, in his opinion, than the mainland province of Cathay. Part of it was called by them Avan (from which the Spaniards later took the name *La Habana* for a settlement there). True, there were no towns or villages on that coast, merely small groups of native houses, but he had continued for many leagues in the conviction that they must soon discover great cities. But because the coastline trended to the north, and winter was coming on, he had turned back and found a marvellously fertile island which he named La Isla Española, with great, gold-bearing rivers, many spices, and large mines for gold and other metals. He described the natives, their amiability, their great canoes made out of a single tree-trunk holding as many as 80 men; that their women appeared to work more than the men; that while in general a man might have only one woman, the chief had twenty. On this Spanish island he had taken possession of a 'large town conveniently situated for the goldfields' and also for communicating with the Great Khan, with whom a most profitable trade might be expected. He had named this town Villa de Navidad and built a fort there, manned by a company chosen from his crews, well-armed and provisioned for a year or more. He had made a great friend of the native chief, but even if the latter

88

Columbus's letter of discovery suggested a far higher degree of sophistication among the native rulers of the Caribbean than was the case. This woodcut was used to illustrate the Florentine edition of his letter and shows a civilised ruler, naked natives and medieval ships. Published 1493. *Courtesy of the Trustees of the British Museum*

should change his mind and attack the fort, it would be of no consequence. His people knew nothing of war and went naked, the most timid race in the world. His own small garrison could destroy all the natives in the island. 'There is no danger for them as long as they maintain discipline.'

Columbus could procure for the Sovereigns as much gold as they needed, if he could be given some slight assistance. He could also give them as much as they wanted of spices, cotton, mastic, aloes and slaves, the latter to be taken from the 'idolaters'. Then, as now, slavery was regarded as a bad thing, except of course for criminals, prisoners of war (the common people but not the officers) and, naturally, members of a rival religion or ideology.

Then he added something which he believed to be true. The Lord God granted victory in impossible circumstances to all those who walked in his way, and such a victory he, Columbus, had most certainly won. For although there had been much talk and writing about these lands out to the west, it had all been speculation. Now there was firm evidence. This triumph should be celebrated by both State and Church, for here was news of many people who could be converted to the holy faith and also temporal benefits from which not only Spain but all Christendom could profit.

The Admiral closed with a lie. He dated the message 15 February, 1493, 'off the Canary Islands'. As he had begun the voyage off the Canaries, it was a plausible untruth; but in fact the letter was written off the Azores, which was the best route to take advantage of the wind pattern he had first guessed at and now proved. In a postscript written later he added, 'I went there in thirty-three days and returned in twenty-eight.' Anyone who tried to emulate him by leaving from and returning to the Canaries would meet constant unfavourable winds on the return and probably perish.

But Columbus was not home yet. There were storms still to come and hostile territory ahead.

9
A Royal Return

The storm had not abated when at dawn on 15 February the lookout in the maintop, Ruy Garcia of Santona, saw land to the east-north-east. Optimistically, many believed that it must be the white rock of Cintra, near Lisbon in Portugal, but Columbus thought it must be an island of the Azores group. However, with the storm now screaming at them from the east, they drifted away downwind.

Then they saw another island and managed to crawl into its shelter, so that the seas abated somewhat, and Columbus could go off duty and lie down. His legs were aching from standing on watch for two days and the previous night; he was chilled through by the bitter wind, and weak with hunger. This night at least he could get a little rest. When the caravel anchored in the lee of this island on the morning of Monday, 18 February, the inhabitants told him that this was Santa Maria, part of the Portuguese Azores.

Spain and Portugal were rivals in exploration and trade. The precise boundaries between their sometimes overlapping spheres of interest were currently in dispute; indeed, the Pope was to be brought in to referee a settlement the following year, to be known as the Treaty of Tordesillas. However, the inhabitants of this particular island appeared to be friendly and showed delight when given the triumphant news of the new discoveries far to the west, well away from the Portuguese route round Africa to India. Three of them came out to the caravel in a boat, bringing food and the compliments of the local governor.

All that could be seen of their village was a hermit's chapel, which they said was dedicated to the Virgin Mary. Columbus thought this was a chance to carry out their last vow, which was that they would walk barefoot in their shirts at the first opportunity to give thanks for their survival. The three men who had made the vow got into the caravel's own boat, were joined by half the crew, and set off on their pilgrimage. The rest remained on board, intending to fulfil their vows when the first party returned.

Columbus waited all morning, and when by mid-day they had not returned, he began to get worried. Perhaps their boat had gone on the rocks. He had the *Nina* moved a little, so that from the deck they had a view

ALEXANDER. VI. PAPA. VALENTINVS. HISP.

Pope Alexander VI, mediator between Spain and Portugal at the Treaty of Tordesillas in 1494. *Courtesy of the Trustees of the British Museum*

of the little chapel of Nossa Senhora do Anjos, where the men had gone to fulfil their vows. The *Nina*'s boat was there all right, but then he saw a troop of horsemen ride up, dismount and get into the boat, armed and warlike. They came straight for the caravel.

This was no brush with ill-armed natives in a mild climate. Columbus told his men to take their weapons but keep down, because he intended to ambush the Portuguese. But the latter were equally wary. Their captain, João de Castanheira, stood up in the boat and called out for a safe conduct so that they could talk at ease. Columbus agreed, intending to break his word once he had got the enemy leader on board the caravel. That stratagem did not work: the Portuguese held off at hailing distance. There ensued some angry exchanges in the wind between the caravel and the boat.

Why had none of his men been returned? shouted Columbus. What about their safe conduct? What about the gifts and offers of help? Hadn't this captain sent his compliments to the Spaniards? In a more conciliatory manner, the Admiral referred to the laws of chivalry, which the Portuguese was thereby ignoring, and was he not also offending the King of Portugal, whose subjects were welcome in Spain and her islands? The

Catholic Sovereigns themselves had given him letters of recommendation to all whom he might meet. They had been accepted in all the places where Columbus had been: why not then in Portugal? The Catholic Sovereigns had appointed him Admiral of the Ocean and Viceroy of the Indies, which he had just discovered. They had ordered him to show respect and courtesy to any Portuguese ships he might meet, as the two nations were friendly; if the Portuguese captain didn't believe it, he could come closer and see that he would come to no harm. But he need not think that the caravel was crippled; he, Columbus, still had enough men to sail her back to Seville with the news of this outrage. Then the Portuguese King might rebuke the governor for precipitating a war!

All this bombast, coming from a frail, leaky, weather-ravaged cockle-shell of a craft whose crew had been reduced to three sailors, some gromets (ship's boys) and a few dispirited Indian prisoners, must have seemed comic. Was this the appropriate command for an Admiral of Spain?

The Portuguese replied that they did not acknowledge the sovereigns of Castile, or their letters; if Columbus did not instantly submit and come into port, they would demonstrate the might of Portugal.

Columbus had been away from home and news of what was going on in the world for almost seven months. There might have been a rupture —even war—between the two Iberian seafaring nations. He decided to put on a bold front nevertheless, especially for the record in case of charges later. He called out loudly—mainly to his crew although the Portuguese might also have heard, or subsequently be claimed to have heard—a threat not to leave his ship until he had captured a hundred Portuguese; he'd take them back to Spain and leave the island depopulated.

With a crew of three men and a few boys, this was idle; he had not men enough even to handle the ship properly, for when yet another gale blew up the Admiral himself had to do deck-hand's work. They lost an anchor trying out one anchorage—presumably chafing on the rocks cut the rope—found no shelter when they sailed off to the island of San Miguel, and were forced back again to Santa Maria. And it was cold. In the Indies, Columbus noted, they had always had calm, mild weather; but as soon as they neared Europe, the ocean became stormy. As the wise men among the ancients had proclaimed that the Earthly Paradise lay in the farthest East, this proved that the lands he had discovered were indeed the uttermost East. Already he was rehearsing his proofs, suspecting how many sceptics he might yet meet.

On 21 February he was back at Santa Maria but to a better reception. A boat came out to them that evening, a notary and five sailors being aboard, and as it was late were allowed to sleep in the caravel. The captain of the island, João de Castenheira, had told them to find out for certain where the

Nina had come from (clearly, an illegal voyage to Portugal's African possessions was suspected), and whether Columbus indeed sailed with the King of Castile's commission. Being satisfied, they released the *Nina*'s boat and the sailors who had gone so dutifully to the little chapel of Nossa Senhora do Anjos to fulfil the vows made in the storm. The wind was now blowing strongly from the south-west, most favourable for the last lap of the voyage, so although the caravel was short both of ballast and of wood for the cooking fires, Columbus decided to sail at once for Spain. That was on Sunday, 24 February.

On 3 March they were engulfed by yet another storm, so fierce that their sails were torn from the yards and they had to run before the howling winds under bare poles. Once more they all (except the Indians, presumably) made a vow to send one pilgrim, barefooted and in only a shirt, to the Virgin of the Girdle, whose church was at Huelva, near Palos. Once again, Columbus was chosen by lot, which he considered evidence that his own personal vows must be most pleasing to Our Lord. Certainly, they were lucky that night. The thunder cracked and boomed over the whitened sea, lit starkly by lightning. Just in time it showed up the land, a rocky, forbidding coast, cruel both to ships and any survivors from them who might be cast into the waters. They hoisted a rag of sail and, literally for their lives, ran from that coast.

At dawn, they knew that they had exchanged one danger for another. A splendid landmark gave their position exactly: a great white rock, rearing 1,350 feet above the sea, and crowned by a Moorish castle or *castello* captured by crusaders in 1147. Columbus knew it well. It was the Rock of Cintra, near the mouth of the Tagus. They had made landfall in Portugal.

*   *   *

The storm they had so far survived had destroyed a great many local ships. Spanish territory was no great distance away, but in their present state —the *Nina* precariously under-ballasted and threatening to capsize, most of her canvas gone, anchors missing, the crew without the means of cooking warm meals—Columbus saw that he had no alternative but to sail into the Tagus and ask for help. He would have to risk suspicions that he had been poaching in the Portuguese possessions on the African Gold Coast and might have illegal treasure aboard—which would attract all kinds of unwelcome interest, unofficial as well as Royal. He would have to risk the attitude of King John II, whose sponsorship he had originally sought for this voyage, who had turned him down on the advice of many wise and learned men, and who might not fully appreciate being proved wrong. On 4 March, 1493, Columbus entered the Tagus.

He anchored off Rastelo, close to the Portuguese guardship, a large and finely-equipped warship, probably a carrack. This was a point of departure for many of the Portuguese missions of exploration, and Henry the Navigator had built there a special house of prayer for the seamen, called St Mary of Belem. Belem, rather than the almost mythical 'court' at Sagres, was the principal home of the Portuguese venturers. Indeed, the master of the guardship at this time was Bartholomeu Dias, the discoverer of what is now known as the Cape of Good Hope. In his voyage of 1487–88, intended at last to round the southern tip of Africa and so prospect the way east to the Indies, Dias had made the daring decision to sail well out into the Atlantic in the hope of finding westerly winds to get him round. When he made that decision, he was 3,000 miles from Mina, the nearest Portuguese base, and 6,000 miles from Portugal itself. Columbus's brother had been there to watch him sail back with the news and was present when Dias showed the King of Portugal a navigational chart illustrating the discovery. Columbus had made a note of it in his copy of Cardinal Pierre d'Ailly's *Imago Mundi*.

Now, the commander of the armed boat coming over to the *Nina* from the guardship was the same man, Bartholomeu Dias. The two great explorers of the rival routes to *Los Indias*—the Orient—were meeting professionally. Dias could confidently expect to be given command of the much larger expedition, in 1497, which would have India as its goal, but sadly he was to be bypassed in favour of Vasco da Gama, who consequently got the credit for almost everything, including in the popular mind the first rounding of that *Cabo Tormentoso* which King John and his publicists renamed more optimistically 'Cape of Good Hope'.

Columbus eventually was to become a victim of some equally odd aberration, but at this moment he was the newly-successful venturer meeting his immediate predecessor. One would give a good deal to know what they would have said, had they been able to meet privately; as it was, neither was there as a private person: they were representing the rulers of rival nations.

The things they'd got right, and the ones they'd got wrong—those would have been the subjects. Both had gambled on predicting the wind patterns in regions to which no one had ever gone—and had been right. And where they had gone wrong—or at least, might have done better, if . . . That would have been more difficult, and also more useful. Columbus would have complained about the Pinzóns, no doubt of it. And the *Santa Maria* had been a pig. Three caravels were what he'd asked for: they'd given him only two, and that old scow. So the Pinzóns had always swept ahead when they wanted, hoping to make the first historic sighting instead of the man who had thought of it all. On the other hand, that set-up Dias had used—two very small but handy caravels with one disposable supply ship as a floating base and mobile storehouse. For a long, uncertain voyage that had its points. Victuals, trade goods, clothing —many ideas to compare. And climate. Great differences there.

According to Columbus, what was actually said was as follows. Dias began by stating that Columbus must come with him to the King's officers and account for his presence in a Portuguese base. That was normal procedure. Columbus replied that as an Admiral of Castile he was not obliged to comply with any such summons and that in any case he was forbidden, on pain of death, to leave his ship on such an errand. He would act in the spirit of that instruction.

Dias conceded that the Admiral of Castile might send the ship's master in his stead to carry out the formalities. Columbus retorted that, by this reasoning, he might just as well send a gromet. The principle remained. It was useless asking him to send anyone from his ship. He wouldn't do it.

Columbus had now, to his own mind, cut what his countrymen would describe as a *bella figura*. It would read well with the Sovereigns of Castile, too. The boldness paid off, he bragged in his account.

Dias pointed out that he needed to confirm that Columbus came in the names of the Kings of Castile, as their subject, and might at least show him their commissions and letters. Columbus produced them, Dias was satisfied with the Admiral's credentials, and went back to his ship to report to his superior, the captain of the vessel, Don Alvaro de Acuna. This nobleman, the military commander of the guardship, responded by giving Columbus a foretaste of triumph. He came out in state to the weary little caravel, with a ceremonial guard, the blare of trumpets, the squeal of fifes and the roll-and-thunder of drums, to greet the conqueror of the Indies.

Next day, the news was all over Lisbon, and a flotilla of boats and launches, carrying the curious, came to gape in the hope of being invited on board and perhaps seeing the brown-skinned natives brought back from over the vast western ocean, and learning of the discoveries from the lips of those who had made them.

The day after that, a letter came from the King of Portugal, John II, congratulating the Admiral on his success, offering dockyard resources with repairs to the *Nina*, and inviting him to pay a visit. The King was then at Val do Paraiso, a monastery nine leagues out of Lisbon, because there was plague in the city. Columbus wondered about his safety, should he accept; and was right to do so, but he decided that he would have to go, just to convince the King that his voyage had been genuinely to the west, nowhere near the areas of Portuguese influence. Transport was provided and so, on mule back, the Admiral arrived at the Court on 9 March.

He was met with honour, all the noblemen being ordered to greet Columbus and bring him into the royal presence. The King told him to replace his hat and sit down, almost as an equal (the chair, unlike the royal one, had no back to it).

Bertie Sadler of Grand Turk, in
the Turks and Caicos Islands, on
the beach which he believes is
where Columbus first landed in
the New World. *Courtesy Amelia
Smithers*

A coral island viewed from the
sea. *Courtesy Bahamas Tourist Office*

A beach on Berry Isle in the
Bahamas: another possible
landing place for Columbus.
Courtesy Bahamas Tourist Office

A coral island coast, showing the
lagoon with the surrounding reef
beyond. *Courtesy Bahamas Tourist
Office*

VT PELICANVS

King John II of Portugal. Having refused to sponsor Columbus on the grounds that his theory was improbable, it must have been embarrassing to have to welcome back the victorious explorer. *Courtesy of the Trustees of the British Museum*

It must have been an awkward beginning. John II had turned Columbus down on good advice, when everyone else was rejecting him, too. Barros, the Portuguese historian, had recorded of that earlier occasion that 'when the King found that this Cristovão Colom was very proud and boastful in presenting his talents, and more fanciful than accurate when speaking of his island of Cipangu, he had little faith in him.' Now, it seems, he was even more boastful, fancying that he had unchallengeably proved his point.

The King studied the Indians he had brought with him as evidence. Brown skinned, dark haired, near naked in the Iberian winter, they must have been miserable, especially after their experiences in the storm; certainly, these were quite unlike the African negroes from his own possessions. The suspicion that this Italian servant of the Spanish state might have been poaching in Portuguese territory could be dismissed. But Cipangu? Were they Japanese? According to Marco Polo, whom Columbus was so keen on quoting, Cipangu had a rich and advanced civilisation equivalent to that of any European state. But just possibly, they could be from some outlying islands.

The King ordered a bowl of beans to be placed on a side table, then signed to one of the Indian captives that he arrange the beans to show how many islands there were. The Indian grasped what was wanted, and arrange the beans like islands on a map. Presumably Columbus prompted him with what he understood to be their names.

When it was done, as if by accident, a sweep of the King's arm scattered the beans and ruined the pattern. John II then commanded a different Indian to replace the beans; and the result was the same pattern of islands. But as the native went on adding more islands and countries, the King appeared to give up, realising what a vast and wealthy area he had forfeited by not sponsoring the Italian.

Columbus now seems to have taken on an almost insulting tone, dwelling on the fact that the King's advisers had been wrong and he had been right. But those advisers had been highly qualified and could draw on far more practical experience of overseas exploration than could the rival Spanish monarchs. John II withdrew to consult them.

Their advice was decisive: eliminate Columbus before he could pass on his information to Ferdinand and Isabella. Call it the plague. On the whole, the King thought not. These islands were, if his advisers' views of the cosmos were correct, very far from the mainland of Asia, and nowhere near their own interests in Africa and the eastern route to the Indies. Spain should not be stopped but encouraged to follow up the ideas of Columbus. He should be praised, honoured and helped on his way to Castile—the sooner the better.

One point which the King did make worried the explorer seriously. He claimed that Columbus's discoveries were really his, according to the terms of a treaty recently signed, defining spheres of influence. The Italian could answer only that he knew nothing of this treaty; his orders had been to avoid the Guinea coast and he had been careful to do that. The King replied soothingly that no doubt the matter would be amicably settled in due course.

The Queen of Portugal, who was at a nearby convent on the Lisbon road, asked Columbus to visit her and give an account of his explorations, and while he was there John II sent a message offering the Admiral an escort and accommodation on the way if he should prefer to travel overland to Castile. Not unnaturally, Columbus preferred the *Nina*'s deck to the back of a mule; and besides, a return by sea to the port from which he had set out all those months ago, was more satisfying. Admittedly, he had sailed with three ships and would be returning with one, but he could fittingly come in as a conqueror with pavisaded sides and gun salutes.

John II's dockyard had seen to the repairing, ballasting and re-equipping of the caravel still lying at Rastelo. On the afternoon of 13 March the *Nina* sailed for Spain.

At dawn on Friday, 15 March, 1493, they were off the river Saltes. As they crossed the bar they could see the convent of La Rabida, where Columbus had once fretted and argued away an eternity of time. Pennants and flags fluttering, bombards thudding in salute, they came in sight of the church and roofs of Palos, and anchored. The greatest voyage in history had ended.

A few hours later, in the evening, another caravel came up river and also anchored off Palos. It was her home port, too. Martin Alonso Pinzón was a sick man and dying, but he had brought the *Pinta* safely back.

10
Hero of Spain

While still in Portugal, Columbus had sent from Lisbon a letter describing the success of his voyage—one is tempted to call it the Interim Report—and no doubt the idea was to pass on his information to the Spanish sovereigns in case anything awkward should happen to him. Even if he were dead, his achievement would live on.

By the end of the month of March, that letter was in print, in a Latin version, in Barcelona. Shortly afterwards, an Italian translation appeared. Barcelona, in the Kingdom of Aragon, was the winter capital of Ferdinand and Isabella. Columbus made his way there by triumphant overland stages. Presumably he first fulfilled his vows at churches in the local towns of Huelva and Moguer, near his point of return at Palos on 15 March.

Within two weeks he was entering Seville, the capital of Isabella's realm of Castile, at the head of his armed mariners, displaying his captive Indians, samples of goldware from the Indies, the gorgeously coloured parrots, the dogs which could not bark. The ceremonial procession must have resembled more than vaguely an ancient Roman triumph. And that indeed is how Columbus from now on saw himself—as a conqueror. A taker.

A week later he received a letter from Ferdinand and Isabella acknowledging his expedition report, addressing him as Admiral of the Ocean, Viceroy and Governor of the lands he had found in the Indies; and urging him to see if anything could be done in Seville and Castile generally to mount a follow-up expedition as soon as possible. After the years of pleading and mocking rejection, Columbus was tasting victory.

An Italian tutor at the court of Castile, Petrus Martyr Anglerius, wrote in May to a friend that a 'certain Christophorus Colonus of Genoa' had just returned from the 'Western Antipodes'. He had had difficulty obtaining the three ships necessary because the Sovereigns had thought that what Columbus had told them might belong to the realm of fable. In another newsletter written in October, Petrus Martyr added a shade of doubt. This 'certain Colonus' believed that he had sailed, not merely to the Western Antipodes, but to the very shores of India. 'I will not deny this, even though the size of the earth's sphere seems to indicate otherwise.' By the following month, November, he was writing about 'Colonus the discoverer of the New World'. To the day of his death, Columbus would angrily have denied that.

Most people, however, accepted the explanation believed by Columbus, that he had arrived at some undiscovered part of the Orient—the Indies—which owed no allegiance to any Christian ruler. The only man with sufficient independence to have formed an alternative appreciation was Martin Alonso Pinzón, who was not committed to any rigid theory such as that which bound Columbus. That he was of independent mind is clear by his actions. He took the *Pinta* out of the storms which plagued Columbus in the *Nina* by sailing well to the north, making landfall on the Spanish coast north of Portugal at Bayona and sending a message overland to Ferdinand and Isabella at Barcelona, offering to report in person on the results of the voyage. Correctly, by protocol, the Sovereigns replied that they wished the Admiral to report. At this snub, Pinzón sailed south to Palos, where he went ashore and died within the week. His part in the expedition therefore remains unclear, although subsequent law suits by the relatives and friends of both explorers show the depth of feeling concerning the public credit due to one champion or the other.

At a higher level, yet another rivalry was evident. Rumours had reached the Spanish court that John II of Portugal was laying claim to the discoveries made by Columbus (which was true enough) and also that the Portuguese were fitting out an expedition to go there (which was unlikely to succeed because Columbus took some pains to keep secret their position). But the matter was too important to be left to mere chance. The Spanish monarchs got in touch with their man in the Vatican—Pope Alexander VI of the well-known Spanish Borgia family—to arrange a papal ruling in their favour.

Columbus, meanwhile, was working out what should be done in the new lands, how it should be done, who should do it, and under what conditions, having regard to the great temptations presented by large masses of gold in the earth or the rivers. He signed this letter with a quite new kind of signature which, with variations, he continued to use for the rest of his life.

.S.
S.A.S.
X   M   Y
:Xpo FERENS

The last line is a Graeco-Latin form of Cristoforo, the Christ bearer. This presumably identifies the writer as the giant who brings Christianity to places over the water; but the line is occasionally altered to read *el Almirante* (Admiral) or *Virey* (Viceroy). The first three lines, however, remain a mystery. Most attempted solutions offer a Christian reading, but one of them postulates that Columbus was a converted Jew trying in a ferociously rigid Christian state to conceal his origins while at the same time proclaiming them—which seems a fanciful and, if true, dangerous proceeding.

As so often before, there is a vacuum at the heart of the Columbus story—and that vacuum is the man himself.

For instance, Bishop Bartholomé Las Casas, as a child in Seville, saw the captured Indians passing in the street and recalled that his young companions wanted to pinch them to see if they were real. It was Holy Week and the celebrations were 'unforgettable in their novelty and splendour'. But on his way to Barcelona, having received the royal permission to visit the court, Columbus spent one night in Córdova, which he considered his home town in Spain. His old friends were there, his sons were there, his mistress—the mother of one of those sons—was there. The friends and the sons greeted him, but nothing is said of poor Beatriz de Harana. The man who would not publicly recognise her—we can suspect his reasons, but we do not know—had returned from a hazardous and perhaps suicidal voyage as a hero about to be honoured at court. What did she feel? What did she say? Did she perhaps suspect that the man's main preoccupation was to go away again?

Leaving Córdova, the Columbus procession set off over the Sierra Morena for Valencia and the coast road to the winter capital of Barcelona, where they found the court and what seemed like the population of the entire city waiting to greet them. So escorted, they reached the royal palace where Ferdinand and Isabella were in residence. Here Columbus was publicly received and honoured almost as an equal by the two rulers. A tall and well-built man of about 40 but with hair prematurely white, Las Casas says that Columbus looked as impressive as a Roman senator (relying on a description by the royal chronicler Gonzalo Fernandez de Oviedo).

Curious gold objects were shown to the guests on trays carried round by royal servants; similarly, caged parrots were carried round for examination; and the natives, still painted but now half-clothed, stood there silently amid all this majesty, while Columbus held his royal listeners' attention with accounts of his discoveries and with answers to their eager questions.

Pointing to the gold, he assured them that infinite quantities were available in the newly-discovered lands; indicating the Indian captives, he described their innocence and docility and readiness to accept the Holy Faith. At the court of a poor, harsh and often barren country embued with a religion newly victorious over the Moors, this was a heady demonstration of what the future now held for Spain. When the royal choir chanted the *Te Deum* there were tears in the eyes of the two Catholic sovereigns.

Columbus with his sons, Diego
and Fernando, and his mistress,
Beatriz Enriques de Harana.
*Courtesy of the Trustees of the
British Museum*

Nevertheless, mundane matters had to be settled in a businesslike way, to avoid later argument and misunderstanding. Columbus saw that his discoveries must be spiritually legitimised, and indeed, by May the Borgia pope recognised his finding of 'islands towards the Indies' and granted their exploitation to Their Catholic Majesties, provided that 'wise and learned men' were sent there to instruct the natives in Christianity. But how to define the spheres of influence involved between, on the one hand, the Spanish area (largely to the west but also southwards to part of the Canary group), and on the other hand, the Portuguese area (largely southwards, but increasingly, in order to round Africa, trending out westwards into the Atlantic)? Columbus wanted it spelt out in detail because these would be the boundaries of *his* kingdom, from which *he* would draw royalties, and over which *he* would have Viceregal powers.

The pope suggested drawing a North-South line 100 leagues west of the Azores as the border of new territory; all to the west Spain's, all to the east Portugal's. The implications of this can only be studied properly on a globe (maps are distorted, often hopelessly so towards the south).

Strong Portuguese protests (so strong that one wonders what their seamen might not already have seen in the distance) led the following year to the Treaty of Tordesillas (June 1494), in which the North-South line was moved westwards (370 leagues west of the Cape Verde Islands). This was subsequently to make a very great difference to Portugal (and again, one wonders).

The previously agreed financial arrangements were confirmed. The Crown would have a trade monopoly in the new lands and one fifth of the gold found was to be set aside for the Spanish Treasury. Columbus was to contribute one eighth of the expenses and receive the appropriate profit; as Governor he would have the power to appoint all officials, subject to Royal confirmation. He was privileged to add to his coat-of-arms the castle and lion, the emblems of Castile and Leon. His brothers, Bartolomeo and Giacomo (Diego in Castilian), would be entitled to call themselves Don. He received an outright gift of 1,000 doubloons (335,000 *maravedis*) in addition to the 10,000 *maravedis* reward previously promised to the first man to sight the new land. That man had in fact been a seaman of the *Pinta*, Rodrigo de Triana. Possibly Columbus was claiming his own report of a flickering light the night before as the first sighting.

Columbus now rode out with Royalty and was dined by the Grand Cardinal of Spain, Don Pedro Gonzáles de Mendoza. The surviving Indians (most did not take kindly to the sharp worsening of climate) were baptised as Christians, and given Spanish names. No one, apparently, asked awkward questions. A few trifles of gold seemed to have mesmerised everyone. The discoverer had proclaimed that there were actual goldfields and gold to be found flowing even in the rivers. On a vast and tragic scale, the former Genoese seaman and apprentice merchant was acting with all the bold, confident optimism of a modern salesman for time-share apartments on the Costa del Sol.

*   *   *

A new state office had been created, 'Superintendent of the Affairs of the Indies', and the first man in the post (he held it for 30 years) was Archdeacon Juan Rodríguez de Fonseca, an energetic administrator. But the plan now put into operation was the one long thought out and suggested by Columbus: a fleet of 17 ships carrying 1,200 men— gentlemen (who provided their own horses), bricklayers, miners, farmers; and farm animals, and plants, and seed. This was an armada of colonisers. It assembled at Cadiz, where a customs house for the colony was established, and sailed on 25 September, 1493.

Supposedly, the religious motive was to be dominant, and it was stipulated that 'the Indians must be treated lovingly, in order that they may be tamed.' There was a fleet chaplain aboard, Fray Bernado Buil, as well as three Franciscan monks and one Spanish Jeronymite.

Columbus's younger brother Diego also sailed, 'a virtuous man, simple

Juan Ponce de Leon, who later conquered Puerto Rico and discovered Florida, sailed with Columbus on his second voyage. *Courtesy Mansell Collection*

of heart and guileless, who wore the habit of a cleric's, according to the future Bishop Bartholomé Las Casas (whose father and uncle sailed with the fleet). There was a distinguished medical man, Dr Diego Alvarez Chanca, physician to Ferdinand and Isabella; and others who were to make their names later, such as Alonso de Ojeda, the future conquistador, and Juan de la Cosa, the future cosmographer (not to be confused with the ship owner of the same name who had served Columbus as master of the *Santa Maria*). Most of the crews had been recruited in Andalusia, but some had served with Columbus on the first voyage, and there were also a few Genoese, including his childhood friend, Michele de Cuneo. But there were no women. It was an all-male expedition.

11
King Solomon's Mine

The two boys, the sons of Columbus—Diego by his Portuguese wife Felipa, Fernando by his Spanish mistress Beatriz de Harana—stood on the shore at Cadiz that September day to watch their father's fleet of exploration weigh anchor. We know because Fernando tells us so. The journal kept by Columbus of this voyage did not survive, but Fernando kept a copy before it was lost and preserved much of the detail in his own writings. Retracing the course of the first voyage, the ships reached Gomera on 5 October and stayed there some time, provisioning. They gave the lady of the island, Beatriz de Peraza y Bobadilla, a gun salute on arrival. The Admiral's Italian friend, Michele de Cuneo, wrote that Columbus had once been in love with the beautiful widow. Was he still? We do not know. How proud was he to arrive there in triumph? We can only guess. How vital had the love affair once been to the explorer on his first setting out? We cannot tell.

What had happened in the distant islands peopled by naked women? Most accounts we have are very strait-laced. This matter was clearly not of public interest. Only one paragraph by Columbus even hints at possible sexual undertones, although it is treated as a good-natured rough-and-tumble by some of the men playfully chasing some of the native girls. On the other hand, one may infer that the original *Santa Maria* was wrecked, not on a rock, but in the aftermath of an orgy of some kind. Nearby was the place where they had set up their colony, leaving behind an armed, provisioned garrison to seek for gold; and it was there they were returning.

During the days of monotonous duty at sea, how many pictured the delights of their return? And for the new faces—the recently recruited colonists—how many had questioned the veterans as to what the new lands were like, and the people? Winks and nudges, certainly. But also a vision of paradise—warmth and soft winds, no need for clothes, calm, clear coral seas, the fragrant scents off the land reaching to the ships miles out to sea—just as in Marco Polo's description of the golden Orient. After a short time in paradise they would be rich.

The expedition's doctor, Diego Alvarez Chanca, counted 20 days since leaving Hierro, the last of the Canaries, when the pilot of the flagship, eager to claim the reward, cried out, 'Land in sight!' As the day was Sunday, they called it Dominica, and were extremely glad to see it because they were weary of working at the pumps hour after hour on a meagre diet. The Admiral had been steering slightly south of his previous course, to pick up an unknown island rich in gold—according to the natives of Española. The latter island, with its settlement at Navidad, the relief of which was their first priority, was soon to become widely known as Hispaniola. They were now coasting along a chain of islands to the south-east, looking for a harbour. There was no gold, but ample evidence of cannibalism.

Their first unpleasant surprise came when a landing party tried eating a local fruit, which proved to be the source of the poison the natives put on their arrows. Dr Chanca noted that the symptoms were an immediate swelling of the face accompanied by pain so unbearable that the men nearly went out of their minds; the cure was cold compresses.

The next sinister discovery, made in an abandoned village, was of human leg and arm bones, scraped clean of meat; yet these people seemed to have a higher culture, judging by their houses and other artefacts, than the friendly, peaceful natives encountered on the first voyage. But the people themselves could not be told apart, at this time, by the novice colonists. Friend or ferocious foe, all seemed alike. In any case, almost all the inhabitants fled at the sight of the ships with great white wings which drifted like a cloud before the breeze past their shores.

On the large island which was to be called Santa Maria de Guadalupe, the Admiral sent many search parties ashore, one of which got lost for four days in the forest of tall trees which blotted out all the sky signs which might have brought them back sooner. The Spaniards were able to capture, in the main, only boys and women, many of whom had been prisoners of the Caribs. All three boys had been castrated. Telling the women apart was more difficult, until the non-Carib women realised that the Spaniards loathed the cannibals. Then, when the Spaniards brought in more captive women, they would say quietly that this one or that one was a Carib. And they pointed out that the Caribs wore two rings of woven cotton round their legs, which made their calves swell and in their eyes made them appear more attractive.

They said that most of the Carib men were away at this time, raiding among the islands for captives. The youngest and most beautiful women were the main prizes, but any children they might have by a Carib man were destined to be eaten. The boys they castrated and used as servants until fully grown, when they were killed and used as food. The Caribs and their customs made such an impact on the invaders that the area of this whole island chain was later to be called after them. Nor was it long before the two warrior cultures clashed. The results were remarkable.

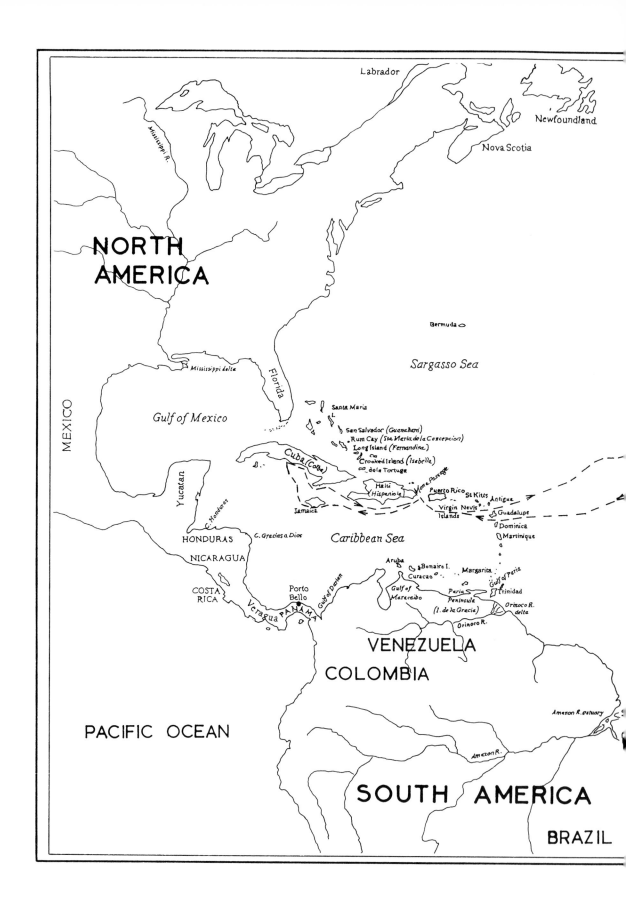

Labrador

Newfoundland

Nova Scotia

NORTH AMERICA

Mississippi R.

Bermuda

Sargasso Sea

Mississippi delta

Florida

MEXICO

Gulf of Mexico

Santa Maria

San Salvador (*Guanahani*)

Rum Cay (*Sta. Maria de la Concepcion*)

Long Island (*Fernandina*)

Crooked Island (*Isabella*)

de la Tortuga

Cuba (*Cuba*)

B.

Yucatan

Mona Passage

Haiti (*Hispaniola*)

Puerto Rico   St Kitts   Antigua

Virgin   Nevis   Guadalupe

Islands

Jamaica

Dominica

Martinique

Honduras

C. Gracias a Dios

Caribbean Sea

HONDURAS

NICARAGUA

Aruba   Bonaire I.   Margarita

Curacao

Gulf of Paria

COSTA RICA

Porto Bello

Gulf of Darien

Gulf of Maracaibo

Paria

Paria Peninsula (*I. de la Gracia*)

Trinidad

Veragua   PANAMA

Orinoco R. delta

Orinoco R.

VENEZUELA

COLOMBIA

PACIFIC OCEAN

Amazon R. estuary

Amazon R.

SOUTH AMERICA

BRAZIL

Map drawn by Maurice Young

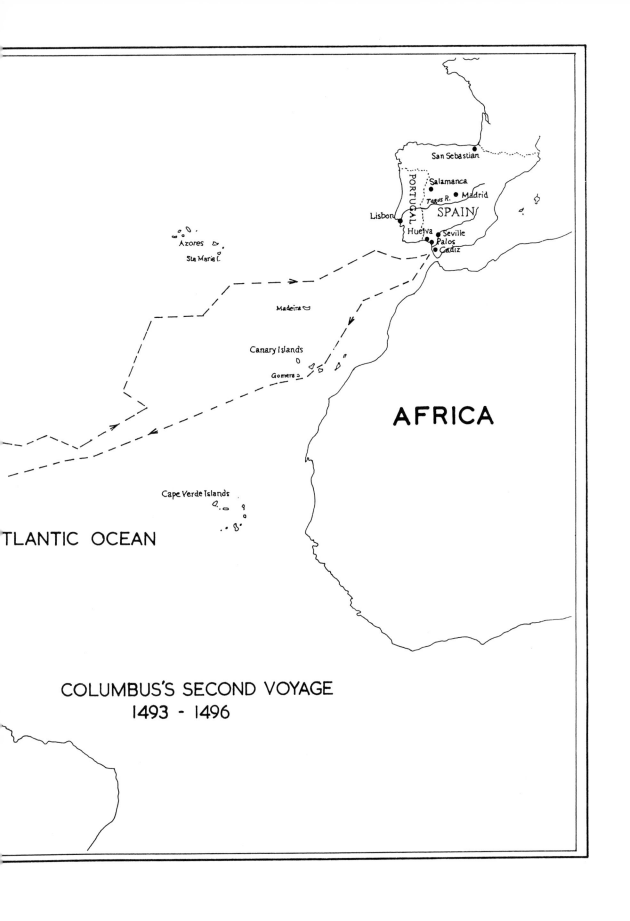

San Sebastian

Salamanca
PORTUGAL
Tagus R. • Madrid

SPAIN

Lisbon

Huelva
Palos • Seville
Cadiz

Azores

Sta Maria I.

Madeira

Canary Islands

Gomera

AFRICA

Cape Verde Islands

TLANTIC OCEAN

COLUMBUS'S SECOND VOYAGE
1493 - 1496

A Spanish landing party of at least 25 men armed with European weapons of steel and iron and protected by wooden shields covered with leather, surprised a native boat crewed by four Carib men and two Carib women. The Caribs, astounded by the spectacle of the Spanish fleet lying there on their waters, failed to see the Spanish boat put off from shore. Outnumbered almost five to one and with only bows and cane arrows tipped by bone or fish teeth—the Stone Age versus the Steel Age—the native warriors and their women should have given in. Instead they loosed a shower of primitive arrows. Most slammed into the hide-covered shields of the Spaniards, but two struck home into flesh—one Spaniard was hit in the side, another pierced through the chest. One of these two, a Basque sailor, died a few days later.

The Spaniards drove their longboat into the light native canoe and overturned it, throwing the Caribs into the water. Some were out of their depth and had to swim, but most managed to reach the shallows, where they could stand, and continue to harass the Europeans with loosed arrows. Some were taken captive, one by then mortally wounded by a spear-thrust. Up to this time, the Spaniards had considered native weapons adequate enough against naked natives, but of negligible value were they to be pitted against European arms and armour.

One of the men in this boat was the old friend of Columbus, his fellow Italian Michele Cuneo. He was given a Carib girl for his pains, and doubtless the Spanish disgust at cannibalism plus the natural arrogance of the victor explains what followed when he got her back to the ship.

> While I was in the boat, I captured a very beautiful Carib woman, whom the Lord Admiral gave to me. When I had taken her to my cabin she was naked—as was their custom. I was filled with a desire to take my pleasure with her and attempted to satisfy my desire. She was unwilling, and so treated me with her nails that I wished I had never begun. But—to cut a long story short—I then took a piece of rope and whipped her soundly, and she let forth such incredible screams that you would not have believed your ears. Eventually we came to such terms, I assure you, that you would have thought she had been brought up in a school for whores.

After the death of the wounded Basque sailor, his body was taken ashore for burial. As far as we know, he was the first casualty of the voyage. They were now off Hispaniola, but a low-lying part not visited during the first voyage in 1492. So large was it, noted Dr Chanca, that it was divided into three native provinces—Haiti, where they now were, and farther on Jamana, and beyond that Bohio. This showed yet again that the Spaniards were consistently misunderstanding the Indian language; it

110

seemed that Haiti and Bohio were alternative words for the whole island, Jamana the local province. Columbus, for one, was beginning to regard their grasp of the language as suspect.

A few leagues short of the stockaded settlement he had left at Navidad in the land of the *cacique* Guacanagari, the fleet found and explored a much better harbour. Men were sent ashore to investigate the possibilities of making a permanent settlement here. The reports were adverse: although a large river with good fresh water led into this anchorage, the surrounding land was marshy, unhealthy and altogether unsuitable. The shore party had also made a sinister discovery—two decayed cadavers.

One corpse had a noose round its neck and the other had its feet tied. In the masses of horrid seething corruption, only these ropes were identifiable. Even if the remains had originally worn clothing, nothing would be visible in the putrescent process now far advanced.

On the following day, going farther upstream along the river bank, the Spaniards found two more corpses. By some freak of corruption not unusual in such cases, the face of one carcase still retained evidence that this man had been bearded. As the veterans of the first voyage said, they had never seen a native with a beard. This man at least was a comrade, and possibly the three others also.

Fearing the rocky shallows which had claimed the *Santa Maria* of the first voyage, they anchored for the night off Navidad, and in the morning fired two bombards to alert the garrison. There were no answering gunshots from the shore. And no signs of life where the fortress had been erected.

Later a canoe approached, sent out by the frendly chief Guacanagari. It was now dark and the natives in it asked the Admiral to identify himself under a lantern, before they would come on board. That, too, was ominous. Was it that they trusted no European except Columbus personally?

They remained aboard three hours, talking to Columbus and surrounded by the Spanish crew. Their leader was a relative of Guacanagari; when asked how the marooned Christians had fared—36 men under three officers—this native said (or so they understood) that all were well, except for some who had died of disease and others in a quarrel between the Christians. Also, two other kings, Caonabó and Mayreni, had attacked and burned the village; Guacanagari had been wounded in this fight, which was why he could not come out personally to the Admiral. But he might be able to do so next day.

While they waited, Columbus sent a shore party to investigate. They found the site of the stockaded blockhouse a pile of stinking, charred wreckage with some evidence that it had been burned in an attack and not by accident—the shreds of clothes and rags used to fire the thatched roof.

Columbus ordered more men ashore to search the area thoroughly, both

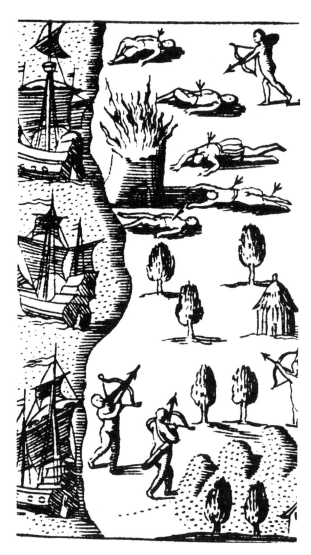

The burning of the settlement of Navidad by the native chief Caonabó, and the massacre of the garrison left behind by Columbus during his first voyage. From a woodcut, source unknown.

around the wrecked stockade and also the burned native village, looking for evidence of what had happened to the garrison and who was responsible. Some of the Spaniards, particularly the Fleet Chaplain, Fray Buil, assumed that the local natives had murdered the Christians and should be rigorously punished. Others, including Columbus, were doubtful.

Proceeding along the coast they came to an intact village. And here before their eyes was evidence: many Spanish articles, including a fine Moorish cloak, unwrapped. No one would have bartered that, they thought. There were stockings and lengths of cloth, too, and also an anchor from the *Santa Maria*. This evidence could be read either way: as booty from the dead or as salvage from the wreck.

Coral reefs are not always visible on the surface. On this one, the upper part is only two or three feet below the surface, but drops steeply to great depths – as much as 6,000 feet. In the days of sail a vessel approaching such a reef could obtain no warning by taking soundings. At one moment, a mile of water under the keel, at the next, nothing, and the ship hard aground. *Photo: Author*

Descendants of the native Caribs still survive in the West Indies, despite the indiscriminate slaughter by the Spaniards. Native hut in the Carib Reserve on the Island of Dominica. *Courtesy COMPIX/Jerry Short*

Statue of Columbus in the
Bahamas. *Courtesy Bahamas Tourist
Office*

Indians from this village began bartering gold, and so many of the Spaniards came back there to trade. Through one of the natives taken on the first voyage and now being used as interpreter, they were shown an area of long grass near the village where lay concealed the bodies of eleven Spaniards. They had been dead less than two months, judged Dr Chanca. To the question, who killed them? the interpreter said it was Caonabó and Mayreni. But, they complained, the Europeans, after Columbus had left, had taken three or four women each for themselves. That, thought the Spaniards, pointed to the oldest motive of all for murder.

From another relative of Guacanagari, who came up to a search party looking for papers and other identification material, they received a much more informed view, for he knew the names of many of the missing Spaniards. As soon as Columbus had left, he said, the colonists had begun to quarrel among themselves. Each man had taken as many women and as much gold for himself as he could get. As a result of this behaviour, Pedro Gutiérrez and Rodrigo de Escobedo had killed another Spaniard named Jácome. That was thoroughly believable. Gutiérrez and Escobedo were two of the three officers left behind in charge of the garrison, Diego de Harana, the Provost Marshal, being the third. Apparently, the task of keeping order had been too much for them, or they had been overcome by the greed for gold and other passions. According to the native, these two officers, with nine others, had gone off with their women to the land of the *cacique* Caonabó, who controlled the area where the gold mines were. Caonabó had reacted by killing them all, and then advanced on the stockade of Navidad. The little blockhouse, with its bombards, was held by only ten men under Diego de Harana, for the rest had scattered widely over the island in search of gold.

Caonabó clearly knew about war. He had come up under cover of darkness, when the guns would be useless and the crossbows almost so, and instead of assaulting had fired the settlement. Eight of the Spaniards, with their women, had fled into the sea and were drowned; the remaining three were slaughtered on land. The native did not know the names of these three.

Guacanagari, he said, had fought against Caonabó's tribe in defence of the Spaniards, but had been wounded and forced to retire. This was a good, believable story—to be repeated many times to Spanish colonisers —but for their own peace of mind needed to be checked. So a group of Spaniards, led by the Admiral and accompanied by Dr Chanca and a fleet surgeon, visited Guacanagari, who was on his sickbed. The bed was, of course, a hammock slung inside a dark hut. Columbus said that he had with him men skilled in medicine, and Dr Chanca suggested that the chief come outside into the light where they could examine his wound. Guacanagari limped out, supported by another native, and sat down. The

Spanish surgeon removed the bandage from the chief's thigh, Guacana-gari grimacing with pain, saying that he had been hit by a stone there, a *ciba*. But to the doctors it seemed that the thigh he complained of was no more injured than the other one. Chanca commented that the *cacique* made 'a cunning pretence of being in great pain'. It may be so, but doctors in the armed forces are quick to suspect malingering.

Columbus was still not sure that they had been told the full story of what had happened, though there was certainly evidence that Guacanagari's people had been engaged in fighting with other natives. Some Spaniards, particularly the Fleet Chaplain, Fray Buil, were convinced of Guacana-gari's perfidy and demanded instant vengeance as a warning to the rest. According to Las Casas, the Admiral pointed out that acts of revenge 'would neither bring the dead back to life nor send them unto Heaven—if they were not already there.' Further, the Spanish Crown had sent him out here to set up a colony, not start a war. And a war could only hinder the conversions to the Holy Faith of these native people, 'which was the principal aim of this undertaking'.

The sentiments were unexceptionable, but there were ten Indian women still held aboard the ships, who had been freed earlier from the Caribs and were now, it seems, prisoners of the Spaniards. A few days later they all slipped quietly into the water during the first hours of darkness and began a marathon swim to the distant shore. Four were recaptured by the ship's boats just as they were emerging from the waves after a swim of some one and half miles. The Admiral reacted by going to Guacanagari to demand the instant return of the half dozen females who had got completely away from him and his men. The chief was not there; no one was. Not surprisingly, the natives had fled. The more sanguine Spaniards read this reaction as mere native trickery, confirmation of their belief that Guacanagari's people had murdered their comrades from the previous voyage; Dr Chanca suspected that the escape of the women had been suggested to them by the relative of Guacanagari who had come on board a day or so earlier.

As a coloniser, Columbus had so far met with no great success; perhaps his Spaniards had not deserved it. Had all gone well at Navidad, there would now have been a flourishing Spanish base on this great island, working with the natives through the chiefs and gathering information about the sources of the gold in possession of the tribes. As it was, the Admiral was left with the charred ruins of his first settlement, hung about with the sickly sweet smell of death, and a shoreline abandoned by the Indians. Had he been engaged merely on a casual pleasure cruise, even so the results must have been depressing; in fact he was leading an expensive business venture which was supposed to bring in a fairly quick return of rich profits to his sponsors, and as matters went so far, he was not even going to cover expenses. Where was the wealth of Cathay? Where were the great trading cities, the teeming quaysides spoken of by Marco Polo?

Far from improving, matters only grew worse. Firstly, only two native 'interpreters' were left out of the seven who had been to Castile and come on this return voyage. Five had died on the way, and the two survivors had been very ill.

Then Columbus decided to found a new settlement, to be called Isabella after the Queen, and chose a harbour they had already passed because there was said to be a gold mine nearby. This meant sailing back eastward against the trade winds, a tortuous process. Men began to fall ill until one third of the crews were sick, including Columbus, according to Dr Chanca, who identified three causes: hard work, the rigours of the voyage, and the change of climate. There was, too, the unaccustomed diet of native vegetables, strange fish, and lack of their usual meat. And mosquito bites, of course. Even so, this epidemic contrasted strongly with Columbus's claim of health on the first voyage; but perhaps he was boasting then, polishing the prospectus.

In any event, the narrative of the voyage fell to pieces. Around the end of January he sent a dozen of his seventeen ships back to Spain with glowing reports of imminent gold finds. The natives lacked iron spades, whereas the Spaniards could dig deep. More than fifty rivers contained gold. Soon, Columbus would be able to give Ferdinand 'as much gold as the iron-mines in Biscay give iron'. Dr Chanca departed with this squadron, fully believing the stories passed on to him by some of the exploration parties ashore; and also Fray Buil and most of his fellow monks, affronted at the way matters were being handled.

Columbus blamed the sickness for the failure to sow many crops, but presented an optimistic picture for the future of the colony. 'This land seems wondrously fertile, and will easily be the equal of Andalusia and Sicily insofar as sugar cane is concerned.'

Although Ferdinand and Isabella had given him explicit instructions to see that his men respected the Indians, to treat them 'well and lovingly' and abstain from doing them any injury, the Admiral now decided that these strictures did not apply to the cannibal Caribs. He suggested in his memorandum that a regular trade in captured Caribs should be set up, the ships returning from the colonies to be filled with cannibals who could be sold when they reached Spain.

It became obvious that the wrong sort of people had been recruited for the fleet. 'None of them wish to make their home in these lands,' noted Cuneo. When the workmen and craftsmen fell ill, few of the *hidalgos*—the proud Spanish warrior caste—were prepared to turn to in their place. 'They considered working with the hands a fate as cruel as death, especially since they had hardly anything to eat.' They had not come there to labour but to get rich through the labours of their social inferiors. Nor were they disposed to obey Columbus who in their eyes was not merely a nobody without land and title of his own by right of birth, but not even a Spaniard. A mere foreigner.

The gold—the presence of it and even the absence of it—made the problem impossible of solution. 'We often fished in the rivers, but nobody ever found as much as a grain of gold,' wrote the Admiral's friend, Cuneo. But when natives actually brought in gold objects to barter, the colonists carried on a private trade with them, regardless of the strict regulations laid down. But they could not keep illicit transactions secret for long. 'As long as Spain is Spain, there will never be any lack of informers,' wrote Cuneo. 'So nearly all were exposed, and those who were found guilty were soundly flogged, and some had their ears slit, and others their noses, and it was a deplorable sight.' Natives who thieved from Spaniards were treated not 'lovingly' but in the same way.

While Columbus was ill, there appears to have been a plot against him led by Bernal de Pisa, the Royal Inspector. The Admiral put him under close arrest—fettered, in fact—aboard his own flagship, and ordered all firearms and ammunition to be brought on board also. His flagship on this voyage was another *Santa Maria*, her common name being *Mariagalante*, and possibly twice the size of the first one. The other large vessel was *La Gallega*. They were probably small carracks, comparatively capacious and defensible, unlike the nimble caravels and tiny 'Cantabrian barques' which made up the rest of the fleet.

After sending part of the fleet back to Spain under the command of Antonio de Torres, the Admiral retained five vessels only in Hispaniola —the two ships *Mariagalante* and *La Gallega*, and the three caravels *Nina*, *San Juan* and *Cardera*. The *Nina* was the same vessel in which he had returned to Spain after the sinking of the first *Santa Maria* in these waters back in 1493. Leaving the two largish vessels and the various shore parties, both at Isabella and at a fort well inland which he called Santo Tomás, under the command of his younger brother Diego and other noblemen, he took the three caravels out to sea on a further voyage of exploration. In general, its intention was to forestall the Portuguese in discovering new territory; specifically, its aim was to find out if Cibao, the fabled land of gold, was the mainland of Asia or only a very large island. The Admiral's old belief, that Cibao and Cipangu were one and the same, had since been exploded by learning more about the native language, in which 'Cibao' stood for 'rocky land'.

He was probably glad to leave the sickness ashore, and the intractable problems of colonisation and setting up a government, well behind him; and to be free again in a job he could do superbly. Michele de Cuneo, who sailed with him on this voyage, too, was to write:

There has never been a man so noble-hearted and so proficient in the art of navigation as the said Lord Admiral. For while navigating, he could say, just by looking at a cloud or a star at night, what was going to happen, or if bad weather was to come. He kept his share of the watch, and took his turn at the helm, and when a storm had passed, he set the sails while the others slept.

Making the *Nina* his flagship for the tiny squadron, the Admiral was to need all his skill. There were reefs and sudden shallows ahead and undreamed-of storms. Columbus had been astoundingly lucky during his first voyage to have encountered delightfully calm, mild weather broken by the occasional stiff breeze and rough sea. He had sailed in what we now know to be the middle of the hurricane season and had yet met no hurricane. In centuries to come, whole Spanish fleets were to be thrown ashore or overwhelmed in these waters, with the loss of thousands of lives.

A modern hurricane jingle current in the area goes: 'June, too soon; July, stand by; August, come they must; September, remember; October, all over.' Like much weatherlore, the predictions are not invariably fulfilled; but long experience shows that August and September are likely hurricane months. Up to now, Europeans had lacked that long experience. On 24 April, 1494, Columbus sailed for the goldfields of Cibao with three caravels.

He coasted west along the northern shores of Hispaniola and crossed a stretch of sea to the next mass of land which, on his first voyage, he had been told by the natives was an island but now seemed to him too large to be anything other than the mainland of Cathay. If, as he suspected, Hispaniola was in fact the great island of Cipangu, then everything would fall into place; reality would match the old maps as well as the descriptions given by Marco Polo and the wonders told of by Sir John Mandeville. Therefore, to the first headland sighted Columbus gave the name *Cabo Alfa e Omega*, because he reckoned it must be the dividing line between the end of the Occident and the beginning of the Orient. Then, because the Portuguese had succeeded in rounding Africa by going south, he too sailed south and then west along the south coast of the 'great promontory of Asia'.

Then, misinformed by a mistranslation of some tale of gold to be found on the isle of Babeque, and that Babeque now lay to the south, he duly sailed south—and found an island. It was called Jamaica, not Babeque, and it held no gold, only a host of hostile natives. To the waving of their pagan spears the Christians replied with a shower of European arrows. 'The fairest isle that human eyes have ever beheld,' wrote the Admiral in his report to the Sovereigns on this delightful prospective property.

Nevertheless, he sailed back to the great promontory of Asia (as he thought) and continued coasting westwards to make quite sure. The three caravels found themselves in a shallow seascape broken by innumerable low islands, so many that it was impossible to name them all, and so Columbus called the entire immense bay the *Jardin de la Reina*—the Queen's Garden. He counted 104 islands and recalled reading in the pages of Sir John Mandeville that there were 5,000 islands in the 'Indian sea'.

Questioning local Indians through his sole interpreter, Columbus learned that Magón lay just ahead. That was the native word for the province, and to the Admiral it was clear from his wide reading that this must be the province of Mangi in south China, as described by Marco Polo. The natives virtually confirmed the supposition by adding that the inhabitants of that province had tails, and that was why they wore clothes—to conceal them. By now, Columbus was a confirmed disbeliever in the monsters and mutants supposed to flourish in all the unknown regions of the earth, but surely the fact that the inhabitants of this place wore clothes must mean that they were civilised, as were the natives of Cathay (if not of Cipangu).

Instead of being on the verge of a triumphant discovery, they sailed into a sea of horror. Instead of being of transparent clarity, like glass, the water was white and milky and concealed everything under its surface. No longer could they safely navigate between the reefs simply by looking down at the seabed as if the water were not there. And yet the seabed was treacherously shallow—sounding with a lead-line gave depths of around two fathoms (12 feet). Some of the seamen recalled Arab legends that the edge of the world was fringed by interminable shoals. But by any reckoning, they were in intense danger. It was impossible even to anchor for the flukes simply dragged over the ground without holding. The bottom must be chalk, judged Columbus. So they had to sail on, fearing any moment that they might strike on an unseen reef and be lost like the *Santa Maria* on their first voyage.

Surviving this peril, a shore party encountered Indians, some of whom wore white tunics like their own priests. That could be another proof that this was the province of Mangi in Cathay, for Marco Polo had written of the Priest-King, Prester John, whose realm was next the great wall of China.

Next day, following up this report, a shore party found the tracks of animals so large that they could only be those of griffins and lions. Mandeville himself had said that it was in Asia that the griffin dwelt. This enormous creature, he wrote, had the head and wings of an eagle and the hind part of a lion, but eight times as large as any lion and a hundred times more terrifying than an eagle. The men were by then down to a ration of one pound of putrid biscuit and one pint of wine per day, and all may well have been suffering from hallucinations. If they caught a fish, it had to be eaten at once, for everything decayed rapidly in this cloying heat. Certainly, there were no griffins ever to be found in this land; nor were there lions. But if they had indeed sighted griffin-tracks, then, according to Sir John Mandeville, the land of Prester John must be near.

Two years afterwards, while staying in the house of the Spanish chronicler, Andrés Bernáldes, Columbus explained exactly his intentions at this time.

> His wish was to find the city of Cathay in the domain of the Grand Khan . . . a province which borders the lands of Prester John. But I told him that he would have had to sail at least twelve hundred leagues farther to reach it . . . Had fortune been with him, he would have attempted to come back to Spain by way of the Orient, the Ganges, and the Arabic Peninsula; and from there overland to Jerusalem and Jaffa, where he would again put to sea.

The Admiral's original plan, as publicly stated, was simply to 'prove' a rapid, safe route to the wharves and warehouses of China. Bold as that undertaking was, this scheme eclipsed it, for it was nothing less than the circumnavigation of the globe at its almost widest point. Of course, the world according to Columbus was a good deal smaller than the world according to Bernáldes—and the real circumference was something else again. Even so, the boldness of the man's vision was astounding.

In his view, the whole journey could be made under sail, except for one small strip of land separating the Red Sea from the Mediterranean (in modern times linked by the Suez Canal).

Without such optimism, he might never have left Spain, let alone come this far. But optimism and empty stomachs do not go well together. Also, the caravels were leaking, from being run aground now and then, from general wear, and probably from the appetite of the wood-eating *teredo* and other molluscs, which can grow to the length of a foot or more.

On 12 June, Columbus could go no farther. He decided to turn back and asked the crews of all three caravels to ratify the decision, not on grounds of sensible seamanship but because they none of them doubted that this interminable coastline was indeed the mainland of Asia and not an island. This acceptance of failure (for the golden cities of the Indies might lie just around the next headland) had to be made fully and officially in order to justify his act to the Sovereigns; so he set Fernando Pérez de Luna, the secretary who was also a notary public, to 'ask the crews if they have any doubt that this land is the terra firma that marks the beginning of the Indies'. The notary was very firm about it. Anyone who did not sign a deposition would be fined 10,000 *maravedis* and have his tongue cut out.

Ship's boys, who did not have that much money, would be flogged instead, as well as losing their tongues. After all, they had sailed along this coast for 335 leagues; it could well be the mainland. They signed.

Two did not: Michele de Cuneo, Columbus's friend, and a priest; and they were not punished.

The return was long and difficult. The *Nina* went aground, but they got her off. They were struck by a thunderstorm so violent that the scuppers could not void the water from the deck and the pumps could not master the flood below. 'Not a day passes but that we see death staring us in the face,' wrote the Admiral.

On 14 September an eclipse of the sun was predicted for 7.15 p.m. in Munich, south Germany. Local time, where they were, would not be the same as in Munich; by measuring the difference, it might be possible to know how far west they were along a line already known by the height of the sun at mid-day. The measurements made by Columbus were not accurate, but then neither were his instruments. By 29 September, 1494, he was back at Isabella, ill and depressed.

His brother, Don Bartolomeo, was already there having been sent out from Spain with three caravels early in May on a mission of re-supply to the colonists. In the autumn of that year, 1494, Antonio de Torres returned with four caravels, also carrying provisions and other necessary supplies which, for the first time, included women. The lack of these, together with insufficient supplies of meat, wine, and other accustomed Spanish fare, had contributed to the lamentable state of affairs on land. The natives, whom Columbus on his first voyage had reported as so docile and unwarlike that a handful of Spaniards could overawe them, had resorted to guerilla warfare, not unsuccessfully, ambushing and killing invaders.

Worse, Torres brought a letter from the Sovereigns telling Columbus about the new treaty (of Tordesillas) made between Spain and Portugal. The line of demarcation was to run, not 100 leagues westward of the Cape Verde Islands, but 370 leagues west. How did that affect the new discoveries? they enquired. And would Columbus return and report, bringing suitable documentation including maps?

Columbus was probably very ill during this period, both from stress and hardship; but it was also a diplomatic time for delay. The colony was in insurrection, the prospect of gold a long-since faded mirage, the quays of Cathay still out of reach, undiscovered.

With the new year of 1495 came better news. Columbus had ordered a punitive expedition to be launched against the troublesome natives, particularly the *cacique* Caonabó, said by Guacanagari to be the chief who had destroyed Navidad and the garrison left behind after the first voyage. In the spring the Spaniards won a battle and returned to Isabella with a captured king, two chiefs and 1,600 ordinary prisoners. The three leaders were sentenced to be shot with arrows, but in the night they chewed through each other's bonds and escaped.

Five hundred and fifty of the best human specimens were selected to be taken to Spain and sold as slaves. They were prisoners of war and, by the usages of the time, enslaving them was legal; very much as it was in the Second World War, although usually officers were excluded from forced labour in the fields, kitchens and mines.

After the 550 for Spain had been chosen, the remainder were available for any colonist to own; when the local Spaniards had made their selections there were 400 left, unwanted. According to Cuneo, many of these rejected people were women with infants at the breast. Now that they were released, they left their babies lying on the ground and ran off in case the Spaniards changed their minds and claimed them for use. Cuneo sailed with the returning slave fleet and recorded that 200 natives died towards the end of their voyage from the temperate zones to the harsher climate of Spain. Of the survivors, half were very ill on landing. No one was going to make much money by selling them.

The Spaniards captured Caonabó at last by a trick and Columbus beat the natives into submission. His son Fernando Colón was to write that in Cibao, where the gold mines were, everyone over fourteen years of age was to pay, once every three months, enough gold dust to fill one large hawk's bell; and after payment had been made were given a copper or brass token. Any Indian found without a token was punished. But there was little gold, and that to be found only in rivers or old river beds; the labour of collecting it was great; consequently, many were savagely punished, some committed suicide.

During that summer of 1495 the Spaniards discovered near their inland fort of Santo Tomás the gold mines they had long been searching for. Or so at least Columbus said. The Italian author Petrus Martyr Anglerius (often known as Peter Martyr) wrote: 'They found there shafts that had been dug long before. The Admiral thought that he had found in these mines the ancient treasures of King Solomon.' Discreetly, he added, 'It is not my task to decide whether this be true or false.' Columbus made the claim in writing several times: 'Hispaniola, that is to say Ophir . . .' To Ferdinand and Isabella he wrote, '. . . thus Solomon, who sent his ships to the farthest point of the Orient to reconnoitre the mountain of Ophir (and Hispaniola is that very mountain . . .).'

He may well have believed that in these latitudes there must be gold in great quantities, but all his actions, not only regarding the gold, mythical or otherwise, but in the capture and attempted sale of slaves, points to some very strong financial imperative. All these explorations had to be financed in part by himself; and as he had neither rich estates in Spain nor liquid cash, he must have taken out vast loans on the basis that he was

When the natives rebelled because of the labour of panning for gold, the Spaniards restored order by the most vigorous methods—and soon had a guerilla war on their hands. From an engraving by Theodore de Bry, published in *Americae*, pars IV, Frankfurt, 1594. *Courtesy National Maritime Museum*

going to conquer and govern rich territories and claim a percentage of the profits accruing. In no way can the Spanish Crown be blamed. Ferdinand and Isabella—and particularly the Queen—were most understanding. They did not expect an immediate flow of great wealth; nor did they ask for it. Mostly, they seem to have been concerned for the welfare of the Indians, that they should be humanely treated and so in due course converted to a belief in Christianity and the afterlife.

By this time, the colonists knew their Columbus as a boastful windbag, a charlatan promising what he could not deliver. They had thought to find gold by the shovelful, and could only wring a few grains of gold dust out of the natives by punishing and torturing. When he returned to Spain, the Admiral knew that he might be called to account for all his empty promises and failures to perform. His cosmography, even, might be in question. He now took to wearing a new and more modest garb—a robe of coarse wool like a dressing-gown, tied at the waist by a cord—which was the habit of a Franciscan friar (Columbus was a lay friar of the Order). He also let his beard grow long.

In June 1495 he had seen his fleet suffer a disaster in the Isabella anchorage. It was early in the season, but the Indians were agitated by the signs—a thick mist, a ring round the sun, the sea rising to an unnatural height, at sunset the sky blood-red. Something terrible was about to happen, whispered the Indians. They called it a *huracán*.

When the winds and the rains arrived, they tossed trees around like sticks, swept whole villages away. The beached Spanish ships were blown over on their sides. Some of those riding at anchor were driven ashore, anchors and all; and three caravels were swamped and sank. Las Casas was to write that this was God's judgement on the Spaniards for their crimes. The natives had been 'ridden down by horses, cut to pieces by

The *huracán* strikes. The weather was unnaturally perfect during Columbus's first voyage, but from the second voyage onwards his ships were to endure gigantic seas stirred up by winds in excess of 100 mph. From an engraving by Theodore de Bry, published in *Americae*, pars IV, Frankfurt, 1594. *Courtesy National Maritime Museum*

swords, eaten and torn asunder by dogs, burned alive, and subjected to all kinds of exquisite torture.'

Columbus reacted not only with a show of humility but by decisive action. The *Nina* was the only caravel which survived the hurricane, and the Admiral used her as a model to build on the spot a sister ship which he called the *Santa Cruz*, although she soon got the popular common name of the *India*.

At the same time he carried out a survey into the religious beliefs and customs of the natives; in particular questioning Caonabó, the captured *cacique* who seemed exceptionally intelligent.

They did, he learned, have the stone age equivalent of churches—huts in which images were displayed. The most important represented the harvest, the second women in childbirth, the third rain and sun. In short, fertility worship, known the world over since time immemorial and echoed in advanced religions. Similarly, they believed in an afterlife. There was a certain valley where they could meet their ancestors again, and take wives, and thoroughly enjoy themselves. The parallels with certain intricately developed religions are obvious. To carry on this work, the Admiral encouraged Fray Ramón Pané in his researches. He was the only monk who had remained when Fray Buil and the rest sailed back to Spain in disgust. Buil was a stickler for protocol and had insisted that the language barrier must be broken down before converting the natives, in order that they might understand what they were being asked to believe.

In October of that year, a squadron of four caravels arrived from Spain carrying the Royal representative, Juan Aguado. His mission was diplomatic: to study the colony and the Admiral's handling of its affairs in the light of the unfavourable reports made in Spain by those who had already returned, such as Fray Buil, but not to supersede him or interfere in any way. The rulers were all aware of the distorted tales which can arise from jealousy or pride. Aguado found that the colony was stricken by sickness and disaffection. They all wanted to forget the place and return to Castile—it had become a favourite oath or catch-phrase. Those who were still fit were out seeking gold and slaves.

In the spring of the new year, 1496, the locally built caravel *India* was launched and the *Nina* refitted and caulked. On 10 March Columbus set off with these two vessels for Spain, having appointed his brother Don Bartolomeo Vice-Governor (*Adelantado*) in his absence. The two vessels carried back 225 Christians and 30 Indians, one of them the *cacique* Caonabó. They carried something else as well, the most lasting export from these 'Indies': syphilis.

In this tropical paradise it occurred among the natives only in a mild form, but brought to Europe and spread among European women, the infection had horrifying results. Contemporary historians found that

124

there was no record of this form of venereal disease occurring in Europe prior to 1494, so they assumed that one or more of the early fleets to return from Columbus's discoveries contained the carriers. Possibly it was also part of the general sickness which affected the colonists on the second voyage, in contrast to the first which was so healthy.

The long voyage home lasted three eventful months, with much hardship. The Indian prisoners aboard were in grave danger of being eaten before they sighted Spain. The last sight of their new world had been a landing on the island of Guadalupe, where they had had a clash with women warriors overawed by the thunder of primitive wrought-iron guns.

12
The Gulf of Pearls

Las Casas, the future bishop, had as a child witnessed the entry of Columbus into Seville after his first voyage to reach the Indies. Older now, he also saw the return from the second voyage. The retinue was much the same as on that first thrilling occasion—the Indians, the gold ornaments, the vivid-coloured tropical birds. But the man himself—the Admiral —entered this time not as a conqueror but in drab, modest robes almost like those of a Franciscan friar. Of course, as he pointed out, Columbus was a great admirer of St Francis.

This time, while waiting to be called to Court, Columbus lodged with the curate Andrés Bernáldes who recorded one clue to our understanding of the relationship between Columbus and the colonists. He had not allowed them to help themselves but had put aside the dues owed to the Crown. Objections to paying the Royal tax were to be a constant source of discontent in the Spanish empire through many centuries, the most cunning and intricate evasions being made. One can well believe this to be a factor behind the resentment shown by many of the Spaniards to the Genoese Admiral, in addition to those of class and nationality, potent enough in themselves.

The curate Bernáldes looked with interest at the native trophies—gold masks, collars, crowns—and saw in them 'the figure of the Devil, in the form of an owl or a cat's head'.

Another contemporary historian, Oviedo, who was also a witness, wrote that the faces of some of the returned adventurers were the same colour as the gold they had vainly sought, 'but lacking its brightness'. There had been plenty of mosquitos and malaria. There was as yet no easy gold to be found, and no goldmines; panning in rivers or digging in dried-up riverbeds was required, and then only to produce negligible amounts. And anyway, *hidalgos* did not dig; that was demeaning to warrior gentlemen. The Admiral's claims that Hispaniola was Ophir were but a bitter jest to those who had been there. 'Admiral of the Flies' was the veterans' name for Columbus.

The Andalusian mariners were not of course gentlemen; they were just seamen, like the many Genoese aboard the ships, and not a few of them understood navigation and could read a *portolano* chart. Here, Columbus did himself no service at all by presenting to the Sovereigns a glittering prospectus of the new lands he had discovered. He was well and kindly received at Court, and perhaps the excitement of the occasion emboldened him to claim that, having sailed completely round Hispaniola, he found that it was 'greater in circumference than all Spain, and has a vast population, all of whom should pay tribute.' As a result of Spanish colonisation one-third of its pre-Spanish population were unable to pay any taxes, because they were dead—of disease, bolt, ball, or spear; or savaged by hunting dogs or ridden under the hooves of horses.

This was not what the Spanish Sovereigns had wanted. They had not looked to a quick material return. Indeed, their instructions to the Admiral for his second voyage had been 'to treat the Indians very well and lovingly and abstain from doing them any injury . . .' There was to be no plunder —the Crown had provided many items suitable for barter; the natives were to be treated with respect, and if anyone ill-treated them, then the Admiral, as Viceroy and Governor, should punish him severely.

It is one thing for a ruler to order, another to see the order obeyed. What had altered everything was the massacre by natives unknown (probably Caonabó's tribe, almost certainly not Guacanagari's people) of the Spanish garrison left behind from the first voyage of 1492–93; and they seemed to have asked for what they got. Even so, Columbus had not been the one to urge instant punitive action without proof, but the Fleet Chaplain, Fray Buil, and his followers.

When an atrocity of any kind occurs, retaliation is hard to prevent, and a rapid escalation follows which it is almost impossible to stop—modern times show many examples. A notable sixteenth-century exception was Drake's action during his round the world voyage of 1577–80, when he forbade retaliation against natives who had tortured some of his men they had captured, because the natives had genuinely mistaken them for Spaniards and there was nothing to be gained by bringing up the guns and slaughtering them. But Drake had previously executed his gentleman co-commander and had his crew firmly under control.*

For many reasons, it was to be two years before Columbus was able to sail again, this time with a supply fleet which, as well as carrying European victuals for the colonists, was to explore to the south and west of Hispaniola. In his absence, time had moved on. The Sovereigns were now primarily concerned with obtaining allies against France and were soon to be at war. The Indies were not a priority and Columbus was by now far from being the only man to know the way there. All the shipmasters of the

---

The Queen's Corsair by Alexander McKee (Souvenir Press, 1978) pp 124–27; and Stein & Day, 1979.

second voyage had had to be briefed on the navigation in case they were separated by storm or other calamity.

Moreover, as a direct result of Columbus's achievement and, to a lesser extent, due to the success of Dias to the south, plans for European exploration overseas were under active consideration almost everywhere. Italians were prominent among the practical seamen and explorers, seeking patrons outside their own country. Giovanni Caboto, citizen of Venice, probably born like Columbus in Genoa and like him initially a trader in the Levant, tried the England of Henry VII and got the merchants of Bristol to back a plan to short-change Christopher Columbus by trying exactly the same idea of sailing west to find the east but in a higher latitude, which meant a shorter route and one clear of any interfering Spaniards or Portuguese. He sailed in the *Matthew* on 2 May, 1497, found land out there in a shorter time than Columbus, and was convinced it was Asia. He set out again, this time as Admiral commanding a fleet, with orders to set up a trading factory in the land of the 'Grand Khan'. He found no eastern spices, but a rich, healthy countryside of great forests and rivers and, farther north, ice. He returned in the autumn of 1498, and sailed a third time with results which have not been recorded. Like Columbus, having changed his country, he changed his name—and became John Cabot.

Meanwhile, the Portuguese were planning an attempt to reach India with a fleet, now that Dias had shown that Africa was not in fact attached to a great southern continent and that the way was clear. The overall command was given to Vasco da Gama, but Dias accompanied the expedition for the first part of the voyage and the choice of a new route—far out into the Atlantic to the west to avoid the inshore headwinds —had nothing to do with da Gama, who is popularly credited with everything, including the previous triumph of Dias. This expedition to the Orient was to sail on 8 July, 1497, with Pero d'Allemquer as chief pilot.

Before his third voyage, the rulers of Spain signed a document which was in effect the Will of Columbus, allowing him to leave his one-eighth share of the eventual profits of the Indies to the persons and causes he nominated. The heirs were his sons and brothers; the causes included Genoa and the latent Crusade to conquer Jerusalem.

Six ships were to be outfitted at Crown cost. The Seville agency handling this work was owned by the Florentine banker Beradi, and its manager at that time, the man who with Columbus would actually do the work, was another Florentine, Amerigo Vespucci.

Columbus was to select the crews and passengers. There were to be 333 in all: 40 gentleman volunteers (*hidalgos*, the warrior caste), 100 foot soldiers (the common people), 30 prime seamen, 30 ship's boys (apprentices), 20 gold-sluicers, 50 day labourers, 20 artisans of various sorts, and 30 women. Among the other passengers were to be monks and

The ship sailed by Vasco da Gama on his voyage round the Cape of Good Hope to the Indies in 1497. Based on a contemporary impression (probably inaccurate). *Drawing by Maurice Young*

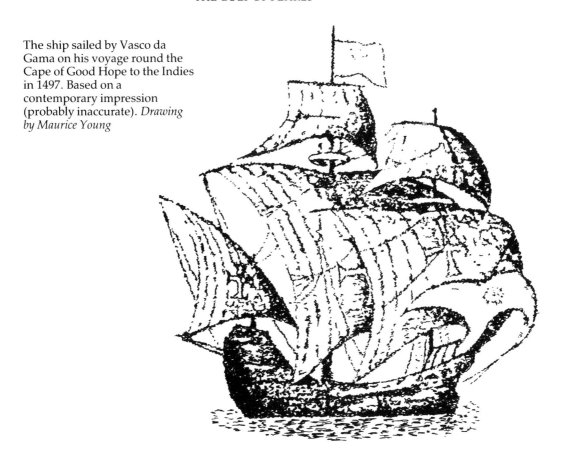

ecclesiastics of proven virtue, a physician, an apothecary, and a herbalist. Recruitment was open to criminals, but only minor offenders would be considered. Those under sentence of death were acceptable (they could serve two years in the colony in lieu) but traitors, heretics, forgers and sodomists were not wanted, nor anyone convicted of stealing gold, silver or copper. It was stressed that the primary aim of the Admiral was 'to lead the Indians to live in peace'.

The flagship of Columbus for this third voyage was the *Santa Maria de Guia*, probably another comparatively capacious *nao*; the *Vaqueños*, a 70-ton caravel commanded by Pedro de Terreros, who had been the Admiral's steward on the first voyage; *El Correo*, commanded by Hernan Péres; and three other vessels of which one was commanded by Alonso Sánchez de Carvajal, a veteran master from the second voyage; another by Pedro de Harana, brother of the Admiral's mistress Beatriz Enriques; and the last by the Admiral's cousin, Giovanni Antonio Colombo, another Genoese. These choices made Columbus an open target for jibes about nepotism, but anyone sailing on such an expedition would positively require a leavening of reliable people in key posts.

All the same, it must have hurt when people passed stinging and 'obscene' remarks in the hearing of his two sons, who had been appointed pages to Queen Isabella. Admittedly, the younger was a bastard, as Columbus still abstained from marrying his mother, Beatriz.

In parallel with scorn and hatred, the Admiral had also become the target of indiscriminate praise. A Catalan cosmographer, Jaime Ferrer, called in to advise the Sovereigns while they were considering the Treaty of Tordesillas, drew their attention to that higher authority, the 'great Admiral of the Indies who knows more of this than any other man and whom Divine Providence has chosen, on account of this great mystery, to make His Glory manifest.'

That was just the trouble. By now, Columbus must privately have been checking and attempting to re-think his original conceptions of geography. Some facts fitted exactly with his ideas: most tellingly, the distance to the 'Indies' he had discovered from his calculated position of Cipangu and Cathay. Other facts did not match at all. There should have been great trading ports with golden-roofed buildings and substantial sea traffic to and from the wharves. Instead, paradisal anchorages unimproved by man and home to primitive natives using stone tools, cane and bone weapons, and living in huts. He must have been an angry, frustrated man at this time. Also, it seems, he had an intuitive feeling that his brother out in Hispaniola was in trouble. He was eager to be away again.

Fitting out the six ships at Seville had taken nearly a year, even with the help of the Florentine, Amerigo Vespucci, with whom he seems to have worked in harmony. Gathering and preserving the cargo of victuals destined for the colony may have contributed to the delay and fuelled his sense of urgency. The two men worked together from 15 April, 1497, to the end of May, 1498, when the fleet dropped down the river Guadalquivir.

Columbus boarded his flagship when it was lying off Sanlúcar de Barrameda, ready for the open sea, on 30 May. Here he acted in a most uncharacteristic way which shocked the Sovereigns when they were told of it. There arrived on his quarterdeck—the fleet's command post—at this most critical time one of the Royal Commissioners, Ximeno de Breviesca, who was an opponent and sceptical of Columbus and his plans, although charged with the duty of seeing the expedition launched. Perhaps he made one malicious remark too many, possibly the Admiral was smarting at the cowardly insults his young sons had to bear at Court; certainly he was under great strain at this moment, and full of excitement and anticipation, too. Whatever the cause, Columbus threw himself in furious outrage on the Royal Commissioner, kicking him, pulling his hair, leaving him disordered, bruised and probably bloodied. He wrote to Ferdinand and Isabella, not to apologise but to ask them not to choose officials

Amerigo Vespucci, who organised the fitting out of the ships for the third voyage on behalf of the Florentine bankers, Beradi. *Courtesy Mansell Collection*

opposed to the project, adding that Ximeno would doubtless be all right, as he belonged to the 'old boy network'.

This was to be a wartime voyage and enemy vessels—the French—had to be looked for. So Columbus changed his route to avoid interception and headed first for Madeira and then for the Canaries, making for San Sebastian on Gomera. As they approached, three ships came out; two were French taking away a Spanish prize. When Columbus sent a fast caravel in pursuit the imprisoned Spanish crew broke out and recaptured their vessel from the French. There is no mention this time of the lady of Gomera. The fleet spent one day provisioning and then went out to sea. A squadron of three supply ships, as planned, steered a course westwards for Hispaniola. The remaining three vessels, with the Admiral, headed south-west to discover rich new lands believed, on the basis of Indian reports, to be found there.

But first the Admiral sneaked a look into the Portuguese zone of exploration. The Cape Verde islands were falsely named, he reported. They were not green but barren and all the inhabitants so sick he dared not stay. The ships then entered a torrid zone of dangerous calms, which spoilt some of the provisions in the holds (recalling the later sailing directions for the route: 'South till the butter melts, then West'). On the parallel of Sierra Leone, Columbus turned west on a route somewhat

131

The discovery of Trinidad, with an inset portrait of Columbus. From a history published in Spain in 1730.

south of that taken on his earlier voyages. On Tuesday, 31 July, a servant of Columbus, Alonso Pérez of Huelva, climbed to the maintop and sighted on the horizon three peaks.

This was a remarkable coincidence, as Columbus had already decided that the first new land they found should be named after the Holy Trinity. And here, the first land had three prominent peaks rising high in the centre. He called it Trinidad.

Columbus had been on the point of heading for the Carib islands, because the ships were short of water, so this new discovery seemed to have been sent from God. He began to explore, landing for water, and learned from the natives that the land beyond Trinidad was called Paria. The natives were if anything fairer even than those on Hispaniola, which surprised Columbus. In common with many learned theorists of the time, and with some evidence from Africa, he believed that the farther south you sailed, so the blacker the skins of the natives became. It was difficult not to accept what at first seemed logical, particularly as there was a linked

132

belief that the farther south you went, and the hotter the climate, the more of the rich metals you were likely to find.

He began to rationalise everything he observed so as to fit the views of the wise and learned. As at this time, and for much of this voyage, he was ill, not only with arthritis but also with some affliction of the eyes which made them bleed, so that he became almost blind, the Admiral's efforts to make sense of what he saw appear startling to modern minds.

The strain of navigating in dangerous and unknown waters must have been considerable, with a multitude of critical decisions to be made daily, often on inadequate evidence. The field of vision from the deck of a small ship is very limited. The squadron entered a gulf between the island of Trinidad and the land of Gracia or Paria, which Columbus thought also to be an island. As they sailed north, Columbus could see lines of waves crossing the estuary with a continual roaring sound, hinting at rocks and shallows, and yet beyond were further areas of broken, roaring water, flowing continually from the west to the east.

If these were shallows, he could not go ahead, so he anchored. While on deck late at night, the Admiral heard a terrible roaring noise approaching from a new direction—the south. The whole sea to the south was rising up in some enormous swell, crested with foam, as high as the ship. For months after, Columbus could recall the physical fear that his ship might be swamped and pushed under when that gigantic swell broke over her in a roaring deluge. Instead, the swell simply lifted the hull into the air and roared into the gulf where it strove with the east-flowing current from the land for a considerable time.

The effect was that of a tidal bore, but the direction was wrong for that explanation; more likely the swell had been formed by some far-off volcanic disturbance under the sea.

Next day the Admiral sent out the boats to take soundings in the area of the lines of roaring waves which seemed to indicate impassable shallows; but it was not so. The shallowest parts were six or seven fathoms down—around 40 feet. And the water was sweet. This must be the mouth of some enormous river.

Columbus was puzzled. At first, he thought he had found only another island. It was in fact the mainland of South America, and the river was the Orinoco. The Admiral's mainland of the earlier voyages—which he had declared was Cathay—lay well to the north and was no continent, merely the large island now known as Cuba. He did not know that, but began to re-think, based on half-learnings and improperly understood religious teachings (as Las Casas was to point out in friendly fashion).

Indians came out to them in canoes, some wearing gold ornaments round their necks, some with pearls tied round their arms. Questioned, they indicated that the gold came from highlands to the west, and the pearls from the west and the north also. Columbus would have liked to explore, but his ship was too large, and anyway the victuals would spoil if he did not reach Hispaniola soon. These natives, too, were light-coloured and friendly. They thought nothing of the trade beads carried in the stores for barter, but they loved the hawk's bells, holding them up and sniffing them (apparently to ascertain what metal they were made of). They valued brass and copper (out of which tools and weapons can be made) above the gold, a soft and largely useless metal in their eyes.

The ships were now penned inside a large gulf, into which a number of vast rivers flowed, blocking the way west. The Admiral tried to escape by rounding the northern headlands. 'I surmised from the ribbons of current and the swelling seas which flowed into and out of these straits with a great roaring of water that there was a battle between the fresh water and the salt.' That much was plain; less clear was the reason for the light colour of the natives' skins and the pleasant climate (rather than the black men and torrid heat the Admiral had expected to find at this latitude).

The Admiral wrote that the world of land and sea was supposed to be spherical, according to the Greek Ptolemy and other authorities, which no doubt was true as far as one hemisphere—the one they knew—was concerned. But he, Columbus, must have now passed into a different hemisphere, unknown to them but now known to him. And this hemisphere, he postulated, was not a perfect match of the other. Rather, it was in the shape of a pear, or a round ball on which was a protruberance something like a woman's nipple. This protruberance was the highest and nearest to the sky. He went on to explain that as the ships sailed west, so they were going uphill and getting nearer to the sky, which was the reason for the light colour of the natives' skins and the pleasantness of the climate. Various philosophers, including Aristotle and a number of Romans, were quoted in support.

From this it followed that the Earthly Paradise must be nearby. In this Our Lord had placed the Tree of Life, whence four mighty rivers flowed —the Ganges in India, the Tigris and Euphrates in Asia, and the Nile which rises in Ethiopia and flows into the sea at Alexandria. Until now, the exact position had been unknown, unstated by writers, not shown on any world maps. But the lake on which his ships were floating was so great that the fresh water had to have Paradise as its source; if not, then the marvel was even greater, for what he had found must then be the greatest and deepest river on earth, and it must come *from a vast land lying to the south, of which we have hitherto had no reports'*. In short: an undiscovered continent.

Columbus was visualising something like Australia lying just off the southern coasts of Cathay. No one then realised the actual nature of what was being seen for the first time, bit by bit and only in comparatively tiny areas of exploration, without any link between them to show that they were continuous. The Admiral's actual words were *que son otro mundo* ('another world'). That was in August 1498.

Columbus was now very ill and could hardly see, his eyes red with blood. After sailing out of the gulf, which the Admiral called the *Golfo de las Perlas* (although they had found no pearls there), into a strait where there were very strong opposed currents, sending up frighteningly high waves so that they called it *Boca del Dragon*—the Dragon's Mouth—the ships came clear of the mainland on their left with Trinidad on their right. The currents and calm weather combined took them gradually out to sea to the north-west, the safest course, until a large island was sighted to the west. By a similar coincidence to that which had given Trinidad so apt a name, he decided to call it the isle of Margarita, after a recently widowed young girl of the Royal family. Then he turned north-east for Hispaniola and anchored off Santo Domingo (which had replaced the now abandoned settlement of Isabella) on 31 August. Margarita, had he known it, was the centre of the rich pearl fisheries later to become famous, employing hundreds of native divers. But he was weary and almost sightless, and besides, the provisions for the colony—corn, wine and meat—were spoiling in the hold. So he abandoned the search for wealth when he was about to make a major discovery.

*　　*　　*

Columbus arrived off Santo Domingo at almost the same time as the three supply caravels he had detached early on his voyage; they had not actually been lost, but Hispaniola is a large island and they were trying to find a settlement which had already been abandoned for a new one. The Admiral's arrival off the western end of Hispaniola (his ships had been offset by a westward-going current) has been acclaimed as a masterpiece of navigation, being, it was said, from one unknown, uncharted point to another. Columbus does not really need uncritical praise as a navigator, since he was ready so often to award it to himself; he was careful always to stress that he was right and every other pilot was wrong, a habit probably due to the practical politics of power, not unknown today in other spheres. No subordinate of the Admiral was likely to be credited with any achievement liable to rival the leader's results. In this case, as Columbus was bleeding from the eyes in most painful fashion and almost blind, surely one of the other pilots in the three ships must be considered responsible for the navigation.

There was no hope of a restful convalescence, however. His brother Don Bartolomeo, the *Adelantado*, or vice-Governor, had grave news. All the Spanish settlers were in a state of great unrest and rebellion; there was an actual revolt in progress, led by Francisco Roldán, the *alcalde mayor*, or Chief Justice; a number of settlers had died and more than 160 were sick

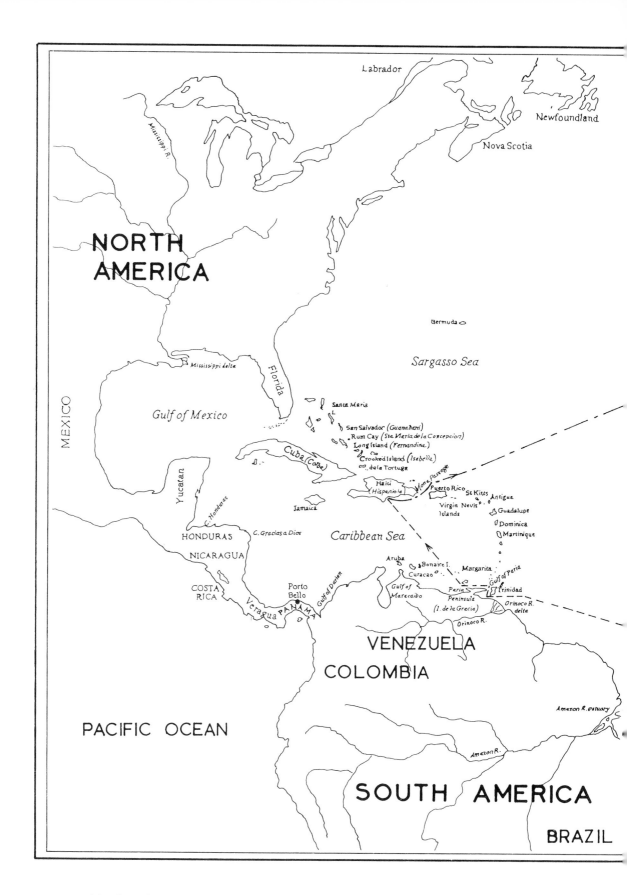

Labrador

Newfoundland

Nova Scotia

Mississippi R.

NORTH
AMERICA

Bermuda

Sargasso Sea

Mississippi delta

Florida

MEXICO

Gulf of Mexico

Santa Maria

San Salvador (Guanahani)

Rum Cay (Sta. Maria de la Concepcion)

Long Island (Fernandina)

Cuba (Colba)

Crooked Island (Isabella)

de la Tortuga

B.

Haiti
(Hispaniola)

Mona Passage

Puerto Rico

St Kitts

Antigua

Virgin Nevis
Islands

Guadalupe

Yucatan

Jamaica

Dominica

Honduras

Martinique

HONDURAS

C. Gracias a Dios

Caribbean Sea

NICARAGUA

Aruba

Bonaire I.

Margarita

Curacao

Gulf of Paria

COSTA
RICA

Porto
Bello

Gulf of Darien

Paria
Peninsula
(I. de la Gracia)

Trinidad

Veragua PANAMA

Gulf of
Maracaibo

Orinoco R.
delta

Orinoco R.

VENEZUELA

COLOMBIA

PACIFIC OCEAN

Amazon R. estuary

Amazon R.

SOUTH AMERICA

BRAZIL

Map drawn by Maurice Young

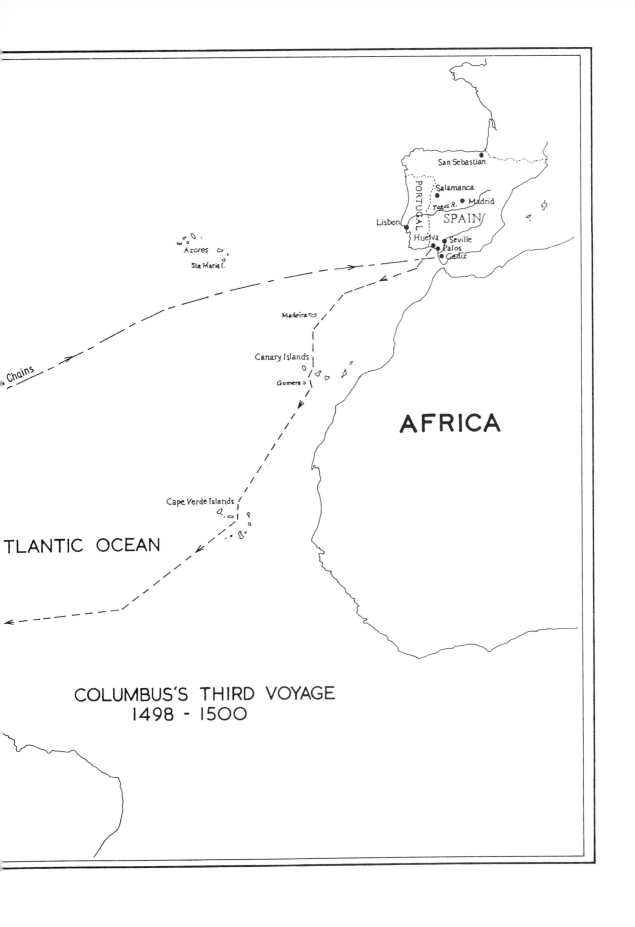

San Sebastian

Salamanca

PORTUGAL

Tagus R. · Madrid

SPAIN

Lisbon

Huelva · Seville
Palos
Cadiz

Azores

Sta Maria I.

Chains

Madeira

Canary Islands

Gomera

AFRICA

Cape Verde Islands

TLANTIC OCEAN

COLUMBUS'S THIRD VOYAGE
1498 - 1500

with the new venereal disease, syphilis, which affected Europeans with horrifying severity. Many Indians were also in revolt, because of the gold tribute they were forced to pay; and a sufficient number of native rebels had been captured to fill the holds of three caravels, now lying in the harbour.

It took a year to sort out all these problems. In the autumn of 1499 the slave ships sailed and Columbus wrote two letters to the Sovereigns, dated 18 October. The first was a report of his explorations along the coast the previous year, near the 'Earthly Paradise', and his amazing speculations concerning the nipple-shaped sphere, and included samples of gold and pearls given to him by the natives. The second letter outlined the lamentable state of affairs in the colony, as seen by the Colón family, and begins to reek with self-pity: It had long been impossible to pay the wages of the colonists and the exaction of a gold tribute from the Indians had had to be abandoned; nevertheless, a new method of making the colony pay had been introduced by allotting to each colonist a certain number of natives to do manual labour for him. This was slavery in the guise of economical management, but Columbus asked that it be sanctioned as a purely temporary measure, for as long as wages could not be paid.

As the returning ships had already been loaded with Indians captured in his absence during the rebellion, the Admiral looked very much on the bright side. He pointed out that it was the custom to use many black slaves in Castile and Aragon, as well as Portugal, Italy and Sicily, and also of course in the Spanish-captured Canary islands. He was quite sure that the supply of blacks from Guinea was beginning to run low. In that context, he made the point that 'a single one of these Indians is well worth three Blacks'. Why, in the Cape Verde Islands, at the start of the voyage, he had seen for himself a bustling trade in slaves, each going on average for a good price of 8,000 *maravedis*. From the two principal products of Hispaniola combined—the slaves and brazil-wood—'one could make a profit of 40 million *maravedis*, so long as there is no lack of ships . . .' Of course, many Indians died on these sea voyages, as had happened at first to the African blacks and Guanches from the Canaries, but it would not always be so, he wrote. The assertion that one Arawak Indian was worth as a labourer three African blacks ought not to be regarded too seriously: Columbus was at that time trying to sell Arawaks in a keenly competitive market and may very well have over-stated the worth of his wares.

It was unfortunate for Columbus that Queen Isabella was present in person at Cadiz when the slave ships were unloaded. All previous consignments had been listed under the heading of prisoners of war, whom it was legal to enslave. But this miserable collection of supposedly hardened warriors included many women and children. Worse, the passengers included repatriated *hidalgos* (including the father of Las

Casas), and a number of these men claimed to own at least one of the slaves on board. Las Casas reported that Isabella asked with fury: 'Who authorised my Admiral to hand over my subjects as chattel to any person whatsoever?'

Columbus knew or sensed that he was being denigrated back in Spain, and wrote to the Sovereigns urging them not to listen to those who tried to stir up hatred against him. Bathed in self-pity, he said that it wouldn't have happened had he been 'a converted Jew, one of those *conversos* who are the sworn enemies of the good fortunes of Your Majesties'; most of the followers of Roldán, he added, were *conversos*.*

A prime objection made by Spaniards against Columbus was that he was a foreigner who surrounded himself with foreigners; and by 'foreigner' they meant Genoese or Italians generally. 'I beg you that no more people of that nation come to these islands,' a Franciscan wrote to the Court.

The pithiest expression of their case against him was recorded by Fernando Colón, while he was still a Queen's page in Granada, in July 1500. A group of repatriated colonists called out to him and his brother: 'There go the sons of the Admiral of the Mosquitos, of the man who discovered the lands of vanity and fraud, the cemetery of Castilian noblemen.'

It was not the whole truth, but so far as it went, it was fair comment.

Columbus was now nearly 50 years old and, despite his tremendous achievement as an explorer, possibly the greatest of all time, he was overwhelmed by the troubles of trying to govern the lands he had found. At Christmas 1499, again according to his son Fernando, his father was attacked both by Indians and by rebellious Christian colonists allied against him, and deserted by everyone. The Admiral fled for his life in a small caravel. 'Then the good Lord helped me, saying: "O man of little faith, fear not, for I am with thee."'

Where Columbus had led, many now followed. And because of his work, they were better informed. Many had been on the Admiral's previous expeditions. An early arrival at Hispaniola, in 1499, was Alonso de Ojeda who had served on Columbus's second voyage; this time he was commanding a fleet. With him was Juan de la Cosa, also a veteran of the second voyage, who was to become a famous cartographer; and a new-comer, the Florentine clerk, Amerigo Vespucci, who was to write a chronicle of this voyage (which either he or his printer was to date earlier than can actually have been the case). Ojeda had been shown Columbus's

*Some scholars—Salvador de Madariaga, for instance—maintain a theory that Columbus was of Jewish origin. It does not seem likely.

Columbus dealt with rebellion among his own colonisers in summary fashion. A visiting inspector from Spain was shocked to find that colonists were being hanged, and removed Columbus and his brothers from their official offices. Engraving by Theodore de Bry, published in *Americae*, pars IV, Frankfurt, 1594. *Courtesy National Maritime Museum*

report and charts of his explorations around Trinidad, Paria, the Earthly Paradise, and Margarita, the island of pearls, which Columbus had never had a chance to investigate; and Ojeda had obtained a permit for his voyage from Don Juan de Fonseca, Dean of Seville cathedral, who had been made responsible for the management of voyages to the Indies.

Ojeda had sighted Trinidad, sailed on to Margarita, found the pearl fisheries of Cubagua and gone into business with the native divers. He went on to explore some new islands and then reached the mainland at a point where a village had been built on piles driven into the seabed of a bay. It was his expedition which noted the parallel and called the place Little Venice—*Venezuela*. Then they turned north for Hispaniola and reached a harbour called by the Indians Yaquimo but which the colonists had named Brazil after the brazil-wood found there. Ojeda picked up a cargo of brazil-wood (theoretically, property of the Spanish Crown) and slaves (forbidden, except in war), and sailed back to Spain. He had certainly discovered a new part of the new continent found by Columbus earlier, but while Columbus merely reported (with charts) to the Sovereigns, the Florentine clerk, Amerigo Vespucci, was to publish. And all else followed.

Other old companions also successfully sought permits to explore and trade. Peralonso Niño of Moguer, pilot of the first *Santa Maria* of the first voyage, who returned with pearls from Cubagua and also gold from farther south. And Vicente Yáñez Pinzón, master of the *Nina* on the first voyage, who led four caravels far down to the south-west, so that he discovered Brazil and the mouth of the Amazon, before heading north to the Gulf of Paria and Hispaniola. Three months later the Portuguese admiral Pedro Alvares Cabrál, with a larger fleet, also discovered Brazil (which protrudes well out into the Atlantic and may have been sighted by Portuguese ships earlier). None of this would have come about but for Columbus.

On 21 May, 1499, the Sovereigns had appointed a successor to Columbus, Francisco de Bobadilla, a senior nobleman, Comendada of the knightly Order of Calatrava; but he did not leave until July 1500, after two shiploads of slaves had arrived to fuel the anger of Isabella at the misgovernment of the colony. Bobadilla may not have known quite what to expect, but when he arrived at Santo Domingo there was plain evidence of turmoil. The bodies of seven hanged men, heads dreadfully aslant, swayed below a gibbet. All were Spaniards. Don Bartolomeo Colón, who was in charge of the settlement, said that the bodies were those of rebels; and five more would join them on the gallows the next day. The Admiral was away, putting down further rebellion.

Bobadilla thought it over for 24 hours, made enquiries, and then acted. He put Don Bartolomeo and Don Diego under arrest and took over the Admiral's residence, impounding his papers and possessions. When Columbus returned, he would not see him but ordered that the Admiral be put in chains.

At first, no one would put the fetters on the Admiral, but then, recorded Las Casas, a common cook of the Admiral's household came forward with a shameless air of impudence, as assured as if he were serving Columbus some savoury dish rather than chaining him.

Columbus became a secret prisoner, and feared execution. Then, according to Las Casas, an equerry entered and commanded the Admiral to follow.

'Vallejo, where are you taking me?'

'Sire, I am taking you to the ship.'

'Vallejo, is this the truth?'

'I swear it on Your Excellency's life it is true that you are going aboard ship.'

All three Colóns were taken together to the ship, through streets covered in abusive placards and filled with a rough mob jeering and blowing horns in triumph as the three captive Genoese were led to the landing stage. Because they might otherwise escape by swimming ashore, Bobadilla had ordered Andres Martin, the ship's captain, to keep Columbus chained until he could be handed over to Don Juan de Fonseca in Seville.

13
'To the Isles Afar Off'

The man in chains wrote not to the Queen herself but to her close friend, Juana de la Torre, who had been governess to Prince Juan, heir to the throne. In this way, he must have thought, Isabella would become aware of his complaints even if only on a semi-official basis.

> Here by God's will I have brought under the dominion of our Sovereigns a new world, whereby Spain, which was called poor, has now become rich. I should be judged as a captain who has borne arms for a long time and bears them still, not laying them aside for a single hour, and I should be judged by knights of conquest and experience, not by lawyers . . . No pirate ever treated a merchant like this!

The caravel was called *La Gorda*. Its captain, Andres Martin, as soon as they were clear of Hispaniola, wanted to release the Admiral from his fetters but Columbus refused. He claimed that as the Sovereigns in their letter of authority had ordered him to obey Bobadilla, only the Sovereigns could unchain him. It was a variant of the public humility he had displayed on the return from the unsuccessful second voyage, by wearing the robes of a simple friar rather than the panoply of an Admiral and Governor. His son wrote that he afterwards kept these chains as relics to remind him how his great services to Spain had been rewarded.

Being extremely self-centred, he wrote too much for his own good. Among his list of complaints was the statement that on his return from exploring Paria he had found 'almost half the settlers in revolt'. That was no advertisement for a Governor who had selected his brother to deputise for him in his absence. Nor was the admission that the settlers were arguing which was best: to search for gold or to go plundering. And that the cost of a woman out there was 100 *castellanos*, the same sum it took to buy a farm; that the trade was common and many merchants went looking for girls: even those aged nine or ten fetched a good price.

On 20 November, 1500, the Admiral could write to his Sovereigns that he had arrived at Cadiz. On 17 December, he and his brother Don Bartolomeo were received by the Court at Granada. Oviedo, the Court historian, wrote that the Admiral went to kiss the hands of the King and

Queen and, weeping, made such excuses as he could. It was a pathetic reversal of his triumphant reception after the first voyage. Bartolomeo was firmer, declaring that he had been injured and despoiled and was unpaid. The King and Queen spoke gently to Columbus, comforting him with assurances that the wrongs would be righted, the revenues and privileges restored; but they did not promise to reinstate him as Governor. Clearly, they were in a delicate position, not wanting to go back on their word expressed in the written contracts; but their erratic explorer, great though his earlier achievements had been, had become an embarrassment. Their decisions were inevitable.

Writing from Valencia on 14 March, 1502, the Sovereigns repeated that they regretted his imprisonment, hoped that he would leave the matter of his estates to be settled with his son, Don Diego, and authorised him to make a further, fourth voyage of exploration to what even Columbus was now calling the West Indies (Vasco da Gama had reached India by the Cape route this same year). On his outward journey he was not to touch at Hispaniola (they had appointed a new Governor, Don Nicolas de Ovando, to replace Bobadilla); he was not to become embroiled with the Portuguese, who were also venturing to India, and he was on no account to bring back slaves. If constrained, on the way back, he could put in briefly at Hispaniola. To the man who had discovered the place, that was a bitter blow; but one can hardly fault the Sovereigns' decisions.

While he was waiting, Columbus embarked on a literary work to explain his holy mission. Aided by a new friend, Don Caspar Gorricio, a Franciscan monk, he assembled an 84-page manuscript called *The Book of Prophecies*, most of which still survives. In the affair of the Indies, it contended, neither reason nor mathematics nor world maps were of any avail; it was necessary, rather, that the prophecy of Isaiah be fulfilled. He may have been thinking of *Isaiah* LXVI, 19:

> . . . and I will send those that escape of them unto the nations, to Tarshish, Pul, and Lud . . . to Tubal and Javan, to the Isles afar off, that have not heard my fame, neither have seen my glory; and they shall declare my glory among the Gentiles.

Some such peal of glory Columbus must have heard long ago, to endure the years of disappointment and the long voyaging. In his haste to secure support now, he cited religious sources to show that the world would come to an end 7,000 years after its Creation. It had been calculated (by King Alfonso the Wise of Portugal) that when Christ was born the world was 5,343 years and 318 days old, so in 1501 only 155 years were left.

Columbus wrote to the Pope to tell him of his voyages and the connection between the riches of his discoveries and the financing of a crusade to

VASCO DE GAMA

Vasco da Gama, who in 1502 completed his voyage round the Cape to India. *Courtesy of the Trustees of the British Museum*

recover Jerusalem from the Moors (the Pope had appealed for a crusade in 1500). A Genoese missionary, Fray Giustiniani, who was then translating the psalter into four languages, added a gloss in the margin of Psalm XVIII.

> Columbus often said that he had been elected by God to fulfil the prophecy of these verses: Their sound is gone out through all the earth, and their words to the end of the world.

On 11 May, 1502, Columbus sailed with four caravels from Cadiz. They were his flagship *La Capitana*, 70 tons; the *Santiago de Palos*, 60 tons, commonly called the *Bermuda* (presumably after her master, Francisco Bermúdes); *La Gallega*, 60 tons; and the *Viscaýno*, 50 tons, whose captain was Bartolomeo Fieschi of Genoa who had known Columbus since boyhood. There were half-a-dozen other Genoese in the fleet.

With him, Columbus carried a Crown letter for Vasco da Gama, in case the two fleets, one Spanish sailing west to the Indies, the other Portuguese sailing east to the Indies, met halfway round the globe. 'You will treat each other in a friendly manner,' ran the instruction.

Two of his relatives also sailed in the fleet, his seaman brother Don Bartolomeo and his thirteen-year-old son, Fernando, who was to describe it in his history. In the four caravels were 140 people in all.

Contrary to his instructions, Columbus anchored off Santo Domingo in Hispaniola on 29 June. He sent his major domo ashore with two messages for the new Governor, Ovando. The first was a request for help, because the *Santiago* was unseaworthy and he wanted her replaced by a better ship. The second was a warning: from years now spent in these waters, Columbus could see that a hurricane was imminent, and he advised that the fleet of 28 ships waiting to sail for Spain should remain in the estuary. Ovando would not be deflected from his orders or his plans, not by Columbus, not by a bad weather warning. Columbus could not have another ship and the cargo fleet, carrying treasure as well as slaves, should leave as ordered. And it did.

Columbus found some sort of shelter in the lee of a small island, but the homeward-bound fleet was caught in open sea. When it was all over, the settlement was an extraordinary sight. 'Santo Domingo, being built of wood and thatch, was laid flat, as if a whole army of demons had broken loose from hell.'

Columbus's four caravels were damaged but still afloat, as were four ships of the 28-strong homeward fleet. All the rest had gone, together with more than 500 people, including the fleet's commander, Antonio de Torres, the former governor Bobadilla who had chained the Columbus brothers, Roldán who had rebelled against Columbus, and a captured *cacique*, Guarionex. Two thousand pounds of gold went down as well, it was said. Three of the surviving ships limped back to the safety of wrecked Santo Domingo, but the fourth, hired by Alonso Sánchez de Carvajal to take Columbus's share of the gold back to Spain, was undamaged and continued her voyage safely.

There were two views on this matter. The friends of Columbus regarded it as divine justice inflicted on his enemies, while the enemies of Columbus alleged that he had raised the hurricane by sorcery. The flaw in these reasonings was that the unfortunate de Torres had been a friend of the Admiral. Very shortly, so consistently bad was the weather on this voyage that the crews of the caravels began to whisper that the ships were bewitched—which was of course a dangerous and heretical opinion. It might be best to call it swings and roundabouts, for on his first voyage the Admiral had been unnaturally lucky with the weather, with sunshine, favourable winds and calm, warm seas all the time, making the discovered islands appear like paradise.

To make matters worse, the 50-year-old Columbus was now ill most of the time—probably with arthritis, possibly gout. He had a little shelter erected on the poop, to keep out the wind and rain while he directed the courses to be steered. For many days at a time, neither the sun nor the stars were visible. What moved him most of all was the distress of his thirteen-year-old son, who nevertheless worked hard. Every man and boy had to hold on with one hand while they worked with the other; with the ships continually in vicious movement, it was impossible to relax or rest; and they all became exhausted.

At the first opportunity they anchored in sheltered water to repair the ships and let the men recover, as well as replenishing supplies of food and water. The local natives spoke an unknown language, so conversation was largely by signs interspersed with the odd word. The land was called Cariai and the natives were friendly, sending out to the ships two naked virgins of about seven and eleven years approximately. Columbus wrote that they behaved so indecently that public women would do no better; and that they had brought sorceress-powders with them. In a fit of decorum or religion, the Admiral had them clothed and returned.

Fernando Colón said that the girls were about eight and fourteen years, and accompanied by an old man with a flag on a pole, a peace emissary of some kind. The girls showed great courage, with no sign of distress or fear, although the European crews must have seemed strange and intimidating to them, and always appeared to be happy and contented. Perhaps they were intended as hostages, a guarantee for the safety of any landing party.

Columbus was now navigating, or rather, trying to map read, from world maps of the Orient, in the still firm belief that that was where he was. He was seeking a way round this awkward territory—huge islands or unknown continent, whichever it was—to reach Chiambra and so into the

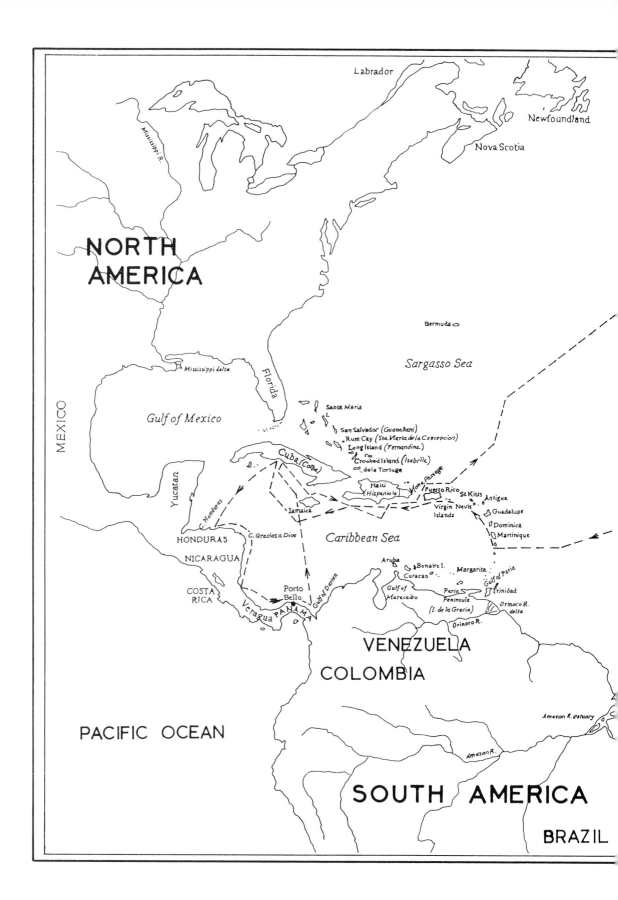

Map drawn by Maurice Young

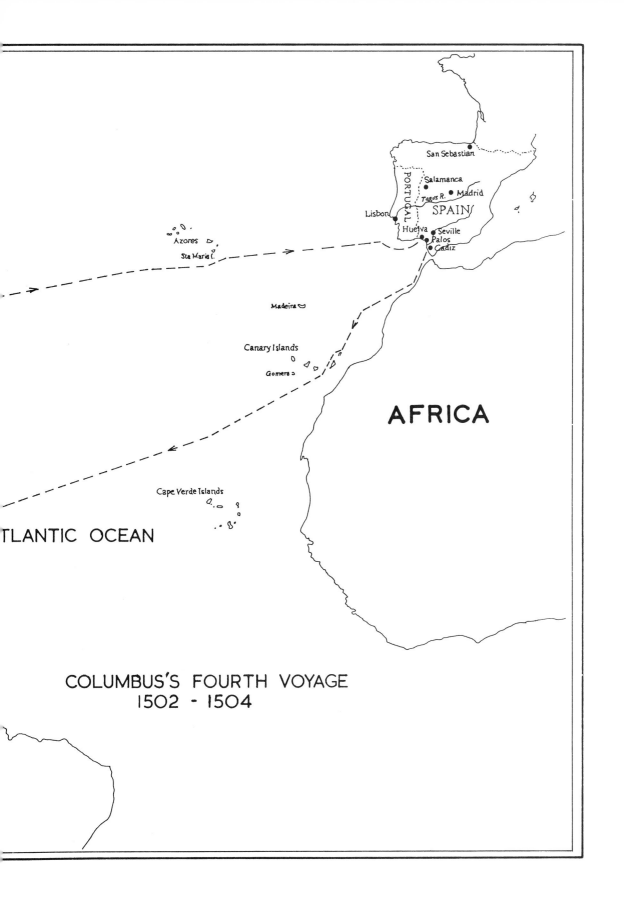

San Sebastian

PORTUGAL

Salamanca

Tagus R. • Madrid

SPAIN

Lisbon

Huelva Seville
Palos
Cadiz

Azores

Sta Maria I.

Madeira

Canary Islands

Gomera

AFRICA

Cape Verde Islands

ATLANTIC OCEAN

COLUMBUS'S FOURTH VOYAGE
1502 - 1504

Indian Ocean, to the gold and jewels of Taprobane (modern Sri Lanka), and a possible rendezvous with the Portuguese fleet of Vasco da Gama.

On 5 October, the four caravels—the submersed parts of their hulls now riddled with molluscs—entered a great lagoon called Chiriqui. Here there were signs of something more than primitive neolithic settlements. So far, the 'gold' ornaments worn by natives had not been pure gold but an alloy of gold, silver and copper called *guanin*. These people wore large discs of pure gold. From his 'interpreter' Columbus learned that in the next province, called Ciguara, the people wore necklaces of coral and bracelets of gold; their chests and tables were layered with gold. Their ships carried cannon and they had the use of swords and horses, they wore rich clothes and lived in good houses. This gold-rich civilisation lay over the hilly interior nine days' journey to the west, where there was another sea. That could only be the Indian Ocean, concluded Columbus: ten days' journey over this sea was the River Ganges. What he was being given, of course, was a description of the Maya civilisation and its people (the guns, swords and horses being wishful interpretation on the Admiral's part to make the tales chime with what was known of the actual Orient).

Farther along this coast called Veragua, he was told, there were more gold mines, and once more Columbus made a positive identification for his Sovereigns. Referring to Flavius Josephus' *Antiquities of the Jews*, he recalled that 'Solomon sent an expedition to look for gold in Aurea. I maintain that the mines of Aurea are these very mines of Veragua, which extends westward for a distance of more than twenty days' journey.'

To back up this contention, he called on the ideas of Marinus of Tyre—'the small earth theory'—as against the rather larger globe of Ptolemy. 'The world is small and six parts of it are land, the seventh part being entirely covered by water . . . the world is not as great as is commonly believed.' You simply had to accept this, if you were to believe that Columbus had now reached Asia, or very nearly. And if he insisted sufficiently often, it would be true: the world could be moulded to his shape.

In December the inquisitive caravels, coasting along the shores of what is now called Panama, were overtaken by another storm. The waves reared high and angry, covered with wind-blown foam, lit the colour of blood by a sky that blazed like a furnace. Lightning flashed vivid illumina- tion of the ominous seas, and then the rain poured down like the Deluge. On the 13th a waterspout menaced the ships, sucking up the sea into the clouds in a dark column as thick as a cask, and twisting like a whirlwind, according to the description given by the young Fernando Colón. 'Just as it passed alongside the ships, the sailors began to recite the Gospel according to Saint John.'

Early in the new year, 1503, Columbus took his leaking, storm-torn

Columbus landing at Veragua, with an inset portrait of his brother Bartolomeo. From a history published in Spain in 1730.

ships into the mouth of a river for shelter. He decided to build a settlement there and called it Santa Maria de Belén. By this time, what with the heat and the damp conditions in the holds of the caravels, the biscuit had become so worm-infested that the men would wait for darkness before eating the porridge made from it, so that they would not see the worms. They had been reduced to eating sharks—quite tasty meat but disturbing to think of—and meanwhile the boring molluscs, probably some species of *teredo*, had eaten the planking of the caravels into honeycombs.

These shellfish, which can grow to a foot or more in length, bore their tunnels lengthways along the planking and never break into each other's tunnels. The caravel in worst case was *La Gallega*, and she was to be left in the river beside the wooden-built settlement. But before the huts could be completed, the level of the river fell so that there was not enough water for them to sail out over the bar. They were trapped.

There was trouble with the natives, too, partly because, as Columbus wrote, 'our men were very peremptory', partly because they were appropriating land for themselves. He managed to get the other three caravels out

151

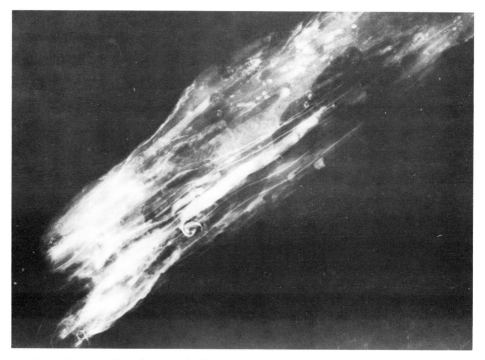

An X-ray photograph of the first plank raised from the Tudor warship *Mary Rose* by the author in 1970, showing an actual *teredo* preserved, probably, from the sixteenth century. *Photo courtesy Central Electricity Research Laboratories*

over the bar at the river mouth by emptying them of their stores and then ferrying these out laboriously in the boats so that the ships were re-stocked and re-armed again, as they lay off.

Left in charge of the settlement with only 20 men was a young gentleman, Diego Méndez. While the bulk of his force were down at the riverside waving goodbye to the Admiral, some 400 natives began to shout threateningly and then assaulted the men around the huts, shooting arrows and hurling darts 'as if attacking a bull', wrote Mendez. Then a storming party armed with clubs attempted to rush them. 'None of them returned, for all lost an arm or a leg or were killed outright by our swords.' The storm party numbered nine or ten, but in accounting for them the Spaniards lost seven men killed. This phase of the fighting lasted three hours, being mainly a fire-fight: natives from the woods loosing arrows and hurling darts, the Spaniards replying with the thundering defiance of their two brass falconets—light infantry guns firing a shot of two pounds or less.

When the battle had died down, Captain Diego Tristán came from the flagship lying off the bar, with a watering party and two boats. Méndez

152

warned him of the danger, apparent from the warlike shouts, trumpeting and drumming being kept up by the natives ringing the settlement; but Tristán over-ruled him and went on to fill the essential water casks. He and eleven of his dozen men failed to survive an ambush, and the boats were lost as well.

Méndez used initiative as well as fine judgement. During a period of four days, while surrounded by hostile natives, he had bags made from the sails of the caravel *La Gallega* and filled them with the remaining supplies of biscuit. Then he improvised what we would now call a catamaran by linking two canoes together with poles, so producing a stable, twin-hulled boat out of two unstable craft, and loading these with the bags of biscuit and casks of wine, oil and vinegar. Then, somehow, when it was calm, this contraption was got out to the ships. In seven journeys all the stores and most of the men, a few at a time, were evacuated. Méndez with five men remained to the last and then got away under cover of darkness. Columbus rewarded him by making him captain of *La Capitana*, the flagship, in the place of Diego Tristán, dead of too much daring.

On 16 April, 1503, the three caravels sailed from the Belén river, and one more bloodily destroyed settlement. After covering 30 leagues it was clear that the *Viscaýno* was becoming so water-logged that she too would have to be abandoned. This was done at Puerto Bello and some 120 men had to crowd into the two remaining caravels, *La Capitana* and the *Santiago*; but it was clear that neither of these would make Spain. All the Admiral could hope for was Hispaniola. He wrote that on 13 May he arrived at the province of 'Mago, which borders on Cathay'. He was referring to the district of Macaca on Cuba, so it seems he still believed (or was still claiming) that Cuba was part of the mainland of China and not a large island, as the natives had reported.

A storm blew up and he anchored in the shelter of an island but the wind must have gone round or the seabed was sharp coral, for he lost three anchors; meanwhile the cables of the *Santiago* parted (again, probably on coral) and she was blown down onto the flagship. When the storm abated, Columbus gave up trying to carry on against the wind eastwards to Hispaniola and just let the two worn-out ships go downwind to Jamaica.

Despite three pumps going continuously in the flagship, spurting water overside, and chains of men baling by hand using pots and cauldrons, the inrush of water could not be kept down. Their companion caravel, the *Santiago*, was so low in the sea as to be almost awash. They ran the two ruined ships ashore on the island of Jamaica, shored them up with posts, and built straw-roofed huts over them, so that they looked like ragged houseboats.

The last of the caravels would never sail again and rescue might be a long time coming, if ever, for there was no gold on Jamaica and therefore no urgent reason for any Spanish ship to venture there. Meanwhile, more than 120 men had to be fed.

In the flagship the young *hidalgo*, Diego Méndez, gave out the last of the wine and biscuit and then, arming himself, with three companions led a reconnaissance patrol into the interior of Jamaica. Instead of a hail of arrows, they met friendly, gentle natives who fed them hospitably. Méndez made a bargain with their chief: the natives would make cassava bread, and hunt and fish, and each day bring the supplies to the ships, for which they would be given trade goods carried in the caravels for that purpose—blue beads, combs, knives, fish-hooks, bells and so on. Méndez then sent one of his three companions back to the Admiral to report the news and arrange the exchange.

He went on to visit a number of other villages, making the same sort of convenient arrangement in each place. On the easternmost cape of the island he made great friends with a chief called Ameyro and from him bought a fine canoe in exchange for a brass war helmet, a coat and one of his last two shirts. The chief loaned him six Indians as paddlers, and in this capacious transport he visited all the other pick-up points, collected the provisions from them, and carried them back to the Admiral. From then on, the Indians brought food to the ships every day.

Ten days later, Columbus drew Méndez aside, and for once we get recalled dialogue from Columbus the commander instead of the written reports intended for Royal eyes. According to the young *hidalgo*, the Admiral said:

'Diego Méndez, my lad, none of my people realise the danger of our situation except you and myself. We are very few, these savage Indians are very many, and we cannot be certain that their mood will not change. One day, when the fancy seizes them, they may come and burn us here in these two ships which we have turned into houses. For since the roofs are of straw, they will easily be able to set them alight from the landward side and roast us all alive. It is true that you have made this arrangement with them to bring us food every day, and at present they are doing so willingly. But tomorrow the fancy may seize them to act otherwise, and supplies will cease. If they do not choose to bring us food, we are not in a position to take it by force. I have thought of a remedy, about which I should like your opinion. Suppose that in this canoe you have bought, someone were to risk making the crossing to the island of Hispaniola, he could there buy a ship in which we could escape from our very great danger. Let me hear your opinion about this.'

The hint was taken. Méndez protested that the project was not merely dangerous but impossible. The Admiral did not deny the difficulties, but said he thought Méndez could do it.

154

The young man pointed out that there were many jealous, proud officers who complained that Columbus favoured Méndez although there were others who could do as well as he if given the chance. So why not assemble everyone and ask for volunteers? If none volunteered—which Méndez expected to be the result—then yes, he would undertake the mission himself.

When volunteers were asked for the result was as expected, although some, as excuse, pointed out that the idea was absurd. To attempt in a small canoe to cross 40 leagues of sea where the currents were powerful and the weather often bad—an area where even large ships had come to grief—was impossible, ridiculous. Not one man objected to Méndez being favoured with this task.

He did not intend to fail for lack of forethought or preparation. He had his canoe hauled up the beach, had it pitched and greased to discourage the 'shipworm', fixed a false keel so that it would not make too much leeway in a strong wind, and nailed some thin planks to bow and stern to increase its freeboard. Then he stepped a mast and shipped a sail, and loaded provisions for eight men—himself, Bartolomeo Fieschi, the Genoese seaman who had captained the *Viscaÿno*, and six Indian paddlers. It was 7 July, 1503. Few of those who watched them go could have expected to see them again.

*   *   *

The hardest thing to do is wait. On 2 January, 1504, about fifty armed rebels swarmed aboard the flagship. They had muttered among themselves that Columbus must have some bad reason for keeping them here—probably he was afraid to return to Spain. These malcontents were led by two appointees of Alonso de Morales, Treasurer of Castile, whom he had forced upon Columbus to please his mistress whose brothers they were. Diego de Porras was along as Royal Inspector, while Franciso de Porras controlled any treasure found and was also the captain of the *Santiago de Palos*.

Columbus, prematurely aged, with white hair, was lying on his sickbed when the rebels boardêd, shouting, 'Kill the Admiral and his men!' and, 'To Castile, to Castile!'

'As God is my witness, I wish this more than any of you,' said Columbus, 'for I am duty-bound to account to God and the Sovereigns for each one of you.'

Shouting 'Let those of you who choose to go to Castile follow me!' Francisco de Porras led his men away. They settled in another part of the island and tried to get away by canoe, but failed. Only 20 healthy men plus a number of sick remained with the Admiral.

155

The following month, his prediction about the natives came true. After seven months of making cassava bread and fishing and hunting for the European castaways, their fascination with the trade trinkets they got in exchange had dimmed. But among the Admiral's books was the *Ephemerides* of Abraham Zacuto, an astronomical almanac which showed that an eclipse of the moon was due on 29 February, 1504.

The Admiral arranged a meeting with all the native chiefs for that night, and warned them that the God of the Heavens was displeased because they no longer supplied the Christians with food; and he would soon show them that displeasure by a sign—he would put out the moon. When the moon began to be covered, the natives were alarmed. With great dramatic sense the Admiral retired to his cabin, turned a sand glass to time the eclipse and, when he judged it was almost over, returned on deck to declare his power to restore the moon to glory if they would continue to supply food. And lo! the moon reappeared. The trick worked, not for Columbus only, but for many a nineteenth century adventure-author wondering how he could rescue his white men from the cannibal cooking pot. Columbus, however, did it first, and in fact, not fiction.

In the following month, March, a tiny vessel arrived from Hispaniola with wine and bacon and a message from Diego Méndez that he was arranging a larger vessel to take them all off. The canoe journey had taken four days and five nights, and cost the life of one Indian paddler who had died of thirst. Méndez had not been allowed to arrange relief for the marooned men but was kept on campaign by the Governor, who was undertaking a punitive expedition which lasted some seven months more. The Governor 'burned or hanged' eighty-four of the leading *caciques*, including the female queen whom they all obeyed, called Nacaona. Only then was Méndez allowed to organise a rescue ship. Columbus and his companions had been marooned for just over a year.

On 28 June they left Jamaica for Santo Domingo, which they reached on 13 August. A month later Columbus and many of his followers (but by no means all) sailed for Spain. They met storms which broke the mainmast in four places; later the mizzen mast fell. It was only on 17 November that they reached San Lucar de Barameda, downriver from Seville, to learn that Queen Isabella was dying, aged 53 (the same age as the Admiral). The Queen had been a prime mover in his series of explorations.

Already Columbus was in a bitter frame of mind, perhaps aware that he had only a few years still to live, and anxious to pass on to his family what profits might still be had from his legacy of the Indies. Before leaving Jamaica he had written a letter to Isabella protesting that he had spent seven years at the royal court, when everyone he met condemned his projected expedition as ridiculous. But now that he had succeeded, 'even tailors are asking for licences of exploration'.

On 3 February, 1505, he received a visit from the Florentine, Amerigo Vespucci, who had sailed under Ojeda to Trinidad and the Pearl Coast, and later gone south for the Portuguese. Two days later the Admiral wrote to his son Don Diego by hand of Amerigo, who had been summoned to Court to discuss questions of navigation, recommending the Florentine as a very honourable man not so far favoured by fortune.

Columbus himself struggled to court in May of that year to argue the case for himself and his relatives, lest they be forgotten in the inrush of newcomers. At this time it was his obsession. At Valladolid the following May his illness worsened and he made his will. On 20 May, 1506, which happened to be Ascension Day, Columbus died, white-haired and worn out by his worries and exertions 'and from the grief of seeing himself so fallen from his high estate'. The man 'not so far favoured by fortune', Amerigo Vespucci, was to reap the harvest of glory which Columbus had sought in vain.

14
In the Wake of Columbus

Just as a great many provinces, cities, towns and villages claimed Columbus dead as their true-born son, so too did scholars innumerable claim this or that island paradise in the Bahamas as the true location of San Salvador, the place of the first landfall of the first voyage. The Bahamas consist of 723 islands or Cays (ignoring the 2,414 recorded rocks), and since 1625 at least nine of them have been publicly proclaimed to be Columbus's San Salvador. In recent times Watlings Island and Samana Cay have been neck-and-neck favourites, with a site in the Turks and Caicos group tending to fall behind in scholarly estimation.

They all look pretty much the same from the sea, and even from the air, and it would be a bold author who expressed a preference. In 1986 the American *National Geographic* magazine argued the case for Samana Cay, thus vindicating President Lincoln's Assistant Secretary of the Navy, Captain G. V. Fox, whose choice of Samana in 1882 had shortly after been supported by a Fellow of the Royal Geographical Society.

The American Admiral (and official navy historian) Samuel Eliot Morison, a long-time student of Columbus, had preferred Watlings—for many years the hot favourite—while the American millionaire inventor of the Link blind-flying trainer, Ed Link, had elected East Caicos. Columbus can have left few if any lasting traces of these early landings to 'take possession' in the name of the Catholic Sovereigns; and even if he had, the chances of identifying and dating them would be as near nil as makes no matter.

Wooden crosses erected on headlands are unlikely to leave identifiable traces after five centuries: a sherd or two of pottery found on some beach—what would that prove? Even under the sea, where preservation is often better, repeated searches in clear, warm water backed up by new high-tech gadgets have failed to find a *provable* Columbus wreck. Scholars have listed 111 ships lost in the New World in the period 1492–1520, and others must have been wrecked unrecorded; but of the few wrecks actually found, none can be precisely identified and dated, let alone hailed definitely as a ship of Columbus, although he left many sunk or abandoned ships behind him. Identifying a wreck can be extremely tricky and the modern underwater explorers have had more than their share of difficulty.

The caravels and *naos* have been called the 'space capsules' of the fifteenth and sixteenth centuries. The search for any kind of historic shipwreck almost anywhere has been likened to a more than usually tedious detective enquiry with only a faint whiff of hazard. It is often said that police investigations which do not very rapidly—within a week or so of the crime—uncover really important clues, are almost bound to peter out. In historical research underwater the crime—possibly a war crime or just a casual moving traffic accident—has by definition taken place a sadly long time ago; in the case of Columbus some 500 years ago.

The first to be wrecked was the *nao Santa Maria*, his first flagship, on a reef off Hispaniola in 1492. Three centuries later a French historian wrote that one of her anchors had been found in a river in what is now Haiti. Perhaps it was the one mentioned by Dr Chanca as being left near the burned ruins of the first settlement at Navidad. But where was Navidad now? In 1939 Samuel Eliot Morison, trying to trace the last voyage of the *Santa Maria*, did not quarrel with his French predecessor's guess. Later, an airman flying over this suspect area saw a vaguely ship-shaped blur underwater inside the outer coral reef; it was anomalous not only because of its shape but because it lay at right angles to the natural lines of the reefs. In 1955 Ed and Marion Link arrived, searching for the *Santa Maria*. They dived and found a very old anchor at another reef near Cap-Haitien which, on being examined, proved to be made of an iron similar to that of the first anchor, on view at the National Museum in Port-au-Prince. Mendel Peterson of the Smithsonian Institution suggested that both anchors might have come from the same ship—the *Santa Maria*. Possibly. But where was the ship?

In 1967 another diving enthusiast, Fred Dickson, set out on the trail of the *Santa Maria*. He knew about the Morison and Link expeditions and conferred with Don Lungwitz, the pilot who had spotted the suspicious ship-shaped mound back in 1949. They located this and began to dig, going down 12 feet (3.7 metres) through coral and ballast rocks to find timber and also fastenings made of copper and of iron, lead sheathing from a hull, and pottery sherds. This neatly illustrated a feature of wooden wrecks in coraline tropical waters: the hull is destroyed—in fact, eaten —by marine organisms such as the *teredo* mollusc, except for the lower timbers covered by the ballast (of rocks, stones or shingle), and then the wreck is grown over, buried and camouflaged by coral so that to a casual eye the site of the lost ship appears nothing more than yet another natural feature of the seabed.

In 1970 a magnetometer—then a new, high-tech gadget, effectively a long-distance detector of some metallic anomalies—was brought in to the search and revealed yet another large anomaly 82 feet (25m) away. When dug, this produced more ship artefacts, plus glass, grapeshot and two pieces of iron ballast found often in warships of periods much later than Columbus. Material recovered the following year had lain in sediments which indicated by radiocarbon dating a wreck some 320 years old. In 1972, death following a diving accident ended Dickson's search for the *Santa Maria*.

She must be an exceptionally difficult site, much of the hull having been removed to build a fort ashore, and much of the contents—including the all-important, tell-tale guns—salvaged and set up in the fort.

In June 1495 a hurricane ravaged the Admiral's new colony of Isabella, destroying at least three ships—although the *Nina* survived to take Columbus back to Spain. In 1980 there were still traces of this settlement mapped by the US Navy in 1891 for the 400th anniversary, as a basis for a seabed search of the harbour and anchorage by high-tech methods in 1983, using sub-bottom sonar as well as a magnetometer. These gadgets are not ignoramus-proof wreck-finders—they merely indicate sub-bottom anomalies. You have to dig to find out what the anomaly is. One anomaly proved to be a modern anchor; another, which was 11 feet 6 inches (3.5m) down, provided only an historical negative: no ship, no artefacts, but a nice mud and silt seabed ideal for preserving ship remains had there been any.

There were no losses on the third voyage but the Admiral's fourth and final visit to the Indies saw the *Gallega* abandoned inside the mouth of the River Belén, the *Viscaýna* at Porto Bello; and at the last, the two remaining caravels run ashore on the coast of Jamaica and turned into beachside forts. It might be thought that two vessels abandoned side-by-side, aground in perhaps less than ten feet of water, would be easy to find; but not so, in spite of many attempts and the use of new high-tech. And surely there would be traces of the settlement ashore? After all, Diego Columbus founded Sevilla la Nueva nearby to commemorate his father's year-long stay on the north coast of Jamaica.

But tropical vegetation, like tropical coral, obliterates or covers man's work. 'New Seville' was not discovered until 1932 when an English plantation overseer, riding through the canefields by the beach at St Ann's Bay, felt his horse stumble. The obstruction proved to be a buried storage cistern, established by C. S. Cotter's excavation of the area as being part of Sevilla la Nueva. The two caravels must be somewhere near, if they had survived.

Between the wars there was renewed interest. In 1935 William Goodwin, an amateur archaeologist, began to dig the first of 150 test holes in Don Christopher's Cove next to St Ann's Bay. All proved blank. Then in 1940, America not then being at war, the Samuel Eliot Morison expedition backed by Harvard University arrived. With Cotter, Morison believed Goodwin had tested the wrong site; they looked at the western end of St

Ann's Bay, where there was deep water next to an old stone wharf, but without success.

In the mid-1960s Robert Marx, an ex-US Marine who was then excavating the very real but supposedly mythical submerged Jamaican 'city' of Port Royal, overwhelmed by an earthquake and tidal wave in 1692, visited Morison's proposed site in St Ann's Bay and his probes produced fragments of wood, stone, pottery and obsidian. In 1968 Marx interested Dr Harold Edgerton, a scientist from MIT Boston, who was developing a range of sonar instruments for commercial purposes but had an intense enthusiasm for historical as well as geological exploration under both the sea and the strata underlying the seabed. 'Doc' Edgerton brought his latest 'pingers' (sub-mud sonars) and the graphs showed two anomalies in St Ann's Bay.

A month or so later the 'Doc' was at Spithead with me, helping with my prospection of a mud and clay seabed for King Henry VIII's vice-flagship, *Mary Rose*, laid down at Portsmouth in 1509, three years after the death of Columbus, and sunk in battle by accidental capsize in 1545. With him he brought the two new 'pingers' he had used with success in St Ann's Bay where, he told me, the sub-mud strata were simple and the anomalies obvious. He found Spithead much more complicated than Jamaica, and could point out four quite different buried anomalies. One of them, I was sure, was the *Mary Rose*, but which one?

What fascinated me most of all, however, was the way that the sonar graphs revealed features buried deep below the seabed, including a mountain, and in another place sediments which Dr Edgerton said must have been laid down in a lake a long time ago, when sea level was much lower. This was real exploration, which one could now hardly do on land, for everything had already been seen and photographed. The 'Doc' had as little interest as I had in space exploration, and truly I rated spacemen only as superior test pilots, not in the same class at all as the captains of the caravels who sailed off into the completely unknown, far from their bases and beyond all help, should anything go wrong.

As it had gone wrong for Columbus on that last voyage, marooning him and his men for more than a year, among natives likely to become dangerous and a crew which could, and did, mutiny.

Marx probed one of the anomalies that Edgerton's pingers had picked up; and found the same materials as before, plus glass, charcoal, flint, an iron tack and a black bean. The datings were not uniform, but this is often the case with a shipwreck, which may include crew souvenirs as well as intrusive material from the surrounding seabed or from fishermen sitting above the wreck. The origins were ambiguous, too, but the same applies, particularly with a returning vessel of exploration. Hopes were now high that one of the two caravels had been found.

The following year, 1969, with the backing of the Jamaican government, test excavations began; the most archaeologically minded of Jacques Cousteau's diving team, Frederic Dumas, was brought in. With much more evidence to go on, Dumas concluded that the wide variety of finds indicated that they were dealing, not with a shipwreck, but a collection of anchorage artefacts lying just off the old stone wharf and dumped overboard or lost by ships lying there to discharge or load cargo.

Starting in 1981, Roger C. Smith and the geologist John Gifford used a mass of high-tech instrumentation designed to trace alterations in the shoreline since the time of Columbus and to explore various sites in the bay. Dumas' conclusions were confirmed, but buried wrecks were found also—all of them decidedly later than the sixteenth century.

The actual ships used by Columbus remain unknown; the documentary and pictorial evidence was always meagre as well as doubtful, which makes the wrecks even more important, and if found, difficult to identify and date.

It would be helpful to know what any caravel looked like, not necessarily a vessel directly connected with Columbus, but certainly from the period of exploration. For this reason the Institute of Nautical Archaeology at Texas A & M University launched a campaign in the 1980s to relocate and properly investigate possible caravel wrecks from that period, which had been discovered by sports or commercial divers since the 1950s. There were only three.

The first to be found appeared as just a small, low mound of ballast stones ten feet down among elkhorn coral at Bahia Mujeres on the Yucatan peninsula of Mexico, shielded by an outer reef. The discovery, which was accidental, was made by José de Jesús Lima, a lawyer, and his sons in 1958. Ed Link arrived with his research ship *Sea Diver* in 1959 and salvaged at least one wrought-iron built-up gun. In 1960–61, the Mexican underwater exploration club CEDAM raised more guns of the same early type, and two anchors. In 1983 INA, with Mexican co-operation, helped record most of the items previously raised and in 1984 surveyed the site. The mound was quite small, 66 feet (20 metres) long. The Valdivia expedition lost a ship in this general area about 1511, but there were other losses later. The remains could not be precisely dated nor a nationality suggested.

The next was also an accidental discovery by a team of three divers in 1965, at Highborn Cay in the Bahamas. The wreck appeared only as a low mound of ballast stones among coral in 20 feet of water. Salvage began in 1966 but was stopped by the government and the finds taken to the United States. INA carried out a reconnaissance of the site in 1983 and three years later began a test excavation which revealed the bottom of the ship lying under the ballast, giving structural information; there were also remains of rigging items, plus rudder pintles. Vicente Yáñez Pinzón lost two caravels in this area in 1500.

The third period wreck lay on Molasses Reef in the Turks and Caicos group of islands—also on a coral reef, also in 20 feet of water, and also with a small stone ballast mound 39 × 10 feet (12 × 3 metres). The find was made in the 1970s and the divers concerned recognised just what sort of guns they were dealing with (although most people would not, because they were covered in a concretion and looked like long, knobbly sausages). All metal objects on these wrecks formed such a natural-concrete covering by the interaction of the sea water with the metals, thus preserving them to a certain extent. If the concretion is roughly or inexpertly removed, any markings on the outer face of the guns go with it; but such markings have been observed and recorded on similar guns from the *Mary Rose*. The INA excavation on the Molasses Reef wreck produced two examples of an early form of musket known as the *Hakenbüchse* or Arquebus, plus two cross-bows. INA consider their wreck as definitely from the first part of the sixteenth century and tentatively from the first quarter.

It was concluded that these early wrecks were small, some 60 to 70 feet long, and carried between 25 and 70 tons of ballast stones; and for their size, heavily armed (although the heavier guns seem to have been stored below on the ballast until needed. This practice was common. For instance, Francis Drake kept the *Golden Hind*'s main armament down in the hold during his circumnavigation of the globe in 1577–80.

The earliest dated and part-identified wrecks found so far are three small merchant ships of the 1554 treasure fleet on its way back to Spain, wrecked on Padre Island, a long sandbank off the coast of Texas. One, possibly the *Santa Maria de Yciar*, was destroyed in the 1940s during dredging operations to cut a channel through the bank; another, perhaps the *Espiritu Santo*, was destroyed in 1967 by a treasure-hunting company, although the artefacts were recovered from the salvors for study. The third, thought to be the *San Esteban*, was excavated in the 1970s for the Texas Antiquities Committee by Carl Clausen and J. Barto Arnold III. Part of the keel and sternpost were the only significant fragments of the hull to be found; the wreck site was represented by a scatter of artefacts lying on a hard clay layer under two to four feet of sand. Secure dating of the last two wrecks was obtained from coins, bullion and navigational instruments.

A recent attempt to find the *Nina* off the Turks and Caicos has failed (1988), but wrecks of the early period continue to be difficult to identify and date even when found in Europe. One example was the so-called Cattewater Wreck off Plymouth in Devon (not Portsmouth in Hampshire, as reported in the USA). Discovered accidentally by dredging in 1973, she was carvel-built and held the remains of a built-up gun as a hint to the period. Another is the so-called Studland Bay wreck, off Dorset, snagged by a fisherman's trawl in 1984 and later excavated. Pottery sherds in numbers were identified as Spanish Isabella polychrome ware datable to around 1480, although the ship herself may be later. But certainly these pieces were made in the reign of Ferdinand and Isabella, who commissioned the four voyages of Columbus.

Details of ship structure, however, as of the guns, do not in the present state of knowledge always make dating easy. For instance, in 1988, I and my friends, excavating a 54-gun ship-of-the-line built in France in 1698 and wrecked on the coast of Sussex in 1706, were puzzled initially by finding long strips of lead which we discovered were used on top of caulking. We had not heard of this type of caulking before, but while researching for this book I came across a reference from Texas—the *San Estaban* was caulked in a similar way and so too, apparently, was one of the early caravel wrecks.

Somewhere, some day, someone will chance upon a caravel of the Columbus period not wrecked on a coral reef but sunk deep into mud with its hull and contents largely intact. Then, and only then, will we be able to see the type of vessel used by the explorers, and visualise the conditions of their daily existence over many months and years.

*   *   *

From the perspective of five hundred years, how should we rate the achievement of Christopher Columbus? The modern reader knows that he did not discover North America (which is what Europeans think of today as 'America'), but he was the first, so far as we know, to sight and land in part of South America (which in his day and for long after was generally thought of as being 'America'). Today we also realise that the bulk of his discoveries were in what we now call, after the original cannibal inhabitants, the Caribbean; that his settlements were in what is now a large island divided between Haiti on the west and the Dominican Republic to the east, and that his supposed mainland of Asia was the large and long island of Cuba. He had not found Japan or any of her outlying islands, and China was not in fact just round the next headland. But he thought so (or said he did).

With Columbus one can never tell. For instance, he tried to show, by citing ancient texts, that the earth's surface is largely land, whereas we now know that it is approximately 70 per cent water, so that from outer space earth, the water planet, looks blue. Did he believe what he said he believed or, like his 'small earth' calculations, was this merely another way of persuading potential backers that his project was practical?

The ancient Greek Eratosthenes, in the third century BC, had calculated the maximum diameter of the Earth to be 27,750 miles, while the Moslem Al-Farghani had in the ninth century AD reached a similar figure of 27,585

164

miles. The actual diameter by modern calculation is 24,902 miles. The world of Columbus was much smaller—18,750 modern miles. By his reckoning (so he said), the distance west from Portugal to Japan was 750 leagues (or 2,760 modern miles). The actual airline distance is some 12,000 miles, impossible for small sailing ships. Had the unsuspected continent of America not been in the way, the caravels of Columbus would have sailed off into the immensity of the Pacific Ocean and all their crews perished of thirst long before an island had been sighted, let alone Asia.

Unluckily for the inhabitants (who were subsequently virtually to be exterminated and replaced by African negroes as slaves), the European explorers proved impossible to curb even by churchmen like Las Casas. One feels that really the Caribs had the right idea about invading Spaniards—they ate them. Not that other European nations were to prove spotless.

The Spaniards did go on to explore and finally conquer the great native civilisations they found on the mainland of South America—the Mayas, the Aztecs and the Incas being the best known. Judged purely as military operations, the achievements of a handful of *conquistadores* were extraordinary. Brazil, which projects eastward into the Atlantic so as to fall within the Portuguese sphere of influence granted by the Treaty of Tordesillas (1494), remained outside the new Spanish Empire.

Columbus's intuition that rich metals were to be found if only one sailed westabout to the Indies proved strangely right. On the mainland of South America, indeed there was gold and a complete mountain of silver. When it was learned that mercury could be used to separate the silver content from baser metals, the mines in South America became a rich reality to the Spanish Crown and very soon, conveniently, sources of mercury also were discovered locally, so that shipment out from Spain became no longer so vital. The fantastic ornaments made out of precious metals by the native civilisations could be taken by the sword and at the urge of market forces melted down to produce coinage—the best known perhaps being the silver 'pieces of eight'. Complete convoys of treasure ships returned to Spain from the New World of the Indies, bringing the lifeblood of Empire. Eventually the 'flota' system included cargoes from the real Indies, the Manila galleons, which crossed the wide Pacific going eastwards to make rendezvous with the other galleons which had yearly collected the treasure tributes from the South American colonies and from the pearl fisheries so nearly discovered by Columbus.

Most of the galleons got through—except those sunk or stranded by hurricanes—because anyone who wanted to hijack Spanish treasure had first to fight a major fleet action with Spanish warships. Spain became the richest Empire on earth. But Spaniards did not become rich. Bitterly, the people referred to the treasures carried back to them by the great 'Plate

Fleet' convoys—the Silver Fleets—as 'raindrops', because in arid Spain the rain instantly soaks away into the soil and vanishes.

Spain's rulers did not use these riches to power a new crusade to recapture Jerusalem from the Moslem infidel, as Columbus had wanted (or so he said, sometimes). But they did employ them for State purposes, for national aggrandisement and the defence of Catholicism against the menace of the Protestant Reformation. A great deal of oppression, bloodshed and torture resulted. Spain conquered Portugal, so that, in theory and in law, the riches of the whole world belonged to Spain, a naturally poor country. Spain tried to hang on to her provinces in the Low Countries, although the Netherlanders revolted against her and were supported by the English. Spain tried, not unnaturally, to make her new empire overseas a trade preserve for Spanish merchants; but could not enforce it. The French, the Dutch and the English burst in. Nevertheless, for good or ill, most of South America today is Spanish speaking.

The man who had touched off these explosive events centuries into the future—Christopher Columbus—did not get the credit. The new continent is not called Columbia—but America, after the man who did not discover it, Amerigo Vespucci, which illustrates the power even then of 'hype'. Like Columbus, he claimed to have made four voyages to the New World. The first and the last are extremely doubtful, but scholars think he may have made two, neither of them in command.

The second voyage (1497–1500) was promoted by Ojeda, and an expedition ship commanded by Vicente Yáñez Pinzón discovered the mouth of the Amazon. Both men were of course already associated with the Columbus voyages, as was Vespucci himself, for he had, as agent for a fellow Florentine, the banker Beradi, fitted out the ships for Columbus's third voyage in 1497–8. Vespucci wrote an enthralling account of his adventures and the sights he had seen during his voyage under Ojeda, but tactfully avoided mentioning the name of Ojeda, who apparently no longer existed—a common ploy even in modern times. In 1507 a German scholar and cartographer, working for Duke René II of Lorraine (probably Martin Waldseemüller), accepted in all good faith the spurious outpourings of Amerigo Vespucci and in admiration suggested that this new continent should be called after its illustrious discoverer, America. And the story was up and running; by 1520 AMERICA was on the maps.

Nowadays we know that the Vikings landed in North America, which they called Vinland, many centuries before; and the Irish claim that a crew of monks also made a successful voyage of discovery in that direction. But the pressure for exploration and exploitation which had built up during the fifteenth and sixteenth centuries makes it certain that, even if Columbus had never existed, some other merchant-mariner would have

Amerigo Vespucci, the Florentine who spuriously acquired credit for the discovery of America, with an array of navigational aids. *Courtesy Mansell Collection*

made the crossing, perhaps promoted by the crown of France or the Crown of England or by the merchant Dutch.

Still, there always has to be a first man who dares, and Columbus should have that status, although it is hard to decide whether or not the Portuguese explorers for the African route to the Indies were not only more successful in their stated aim, but perhaps achieved an equal or even greater feat.

And there is yet another Portuguese explorer, Ferdinand Magellan, who in 1519 led a Spanish fleet from Seville on a voyage to circumnavigate the globe, believing that there was a way round the southern tip of South America. Only one ship returned, under Sebastian El Cano, for Magellan had been killed by natives in the Philippines; but the voyage proved beyond doubt that America was a continent quite separate from Asia, and that the world was a bigger place than many, including Columbus, had thought.

Characters in the Columbus Story

The Columbus Family

Christopher Columbus—adventurer, seaman and chart-maker
  also known as:
  Cristoforo Colombo (Italy)
  Cristovão Colom (Portugal)
  Cristóbal Colón (Spain)
Diego (Giacomo) Columbus (Colón)—legitimate son of Columbus
Fernando Colón—illegitimate son of Columbus
Bartolomeo Columbus (Colón)—younger brother of Columbus, chart-maker in Lisbon
Diego (Giacomo) Columbus (Colón)—brother of Columbus
Dona Felipa Moniz de Perestrello—wife of Columbus, daughter of the governor of Porto Santo and mother of Diego
Beatriz Enriques de Harana—mistress of Columbus, mother of Fernando

Friends of Columbus

Bartholomé Las Casas—later Bishop of the Indies and author of *Historia de las Indias*
Dom Bartholomeu de Perestrello—first Governor of Porto Santo
Juan Pérez—Prior of the monastery of La Rabida
Beatriz de Peraza y Bobadilla—wife of Alonso de Lugo, Governor of Gomera, possible love of Columbus
Michele de Cuneo—Italian, childhood friend of Columbus
Andrés Bernáldes—Spanish chronicler
Juana de la Torre—governess to Prince Juan of Spain
Amerigo Vespucci—Florentine, employed by banker Beradi, later sailed to South America

The Spanish Royal Court

Ferdinand—King of Aragon
Isabella—Queen of Castile
Gonzalo Fernandez de Oviedo—Royal Chancellor of Spain
Don Pedro Gonzales de Mendoza—Grand Cardinal of Spain
Archdeacon Juan Rodrigues de Fonseca—Superintendent of the Affairs of the Indies

Juan de Cóloma—State Secretary of Aragon (*converso*)
Luis de Santangel—financier at the Spanish Court (*converso*)
Ximeno de Breviesca—Spanish Royal Commissioner
Alonso de Morales—Treasurer of Castile
Petrus Martyr Anglerius (Peter Martyr)—Tutor at the Court of Castile
Hernando de Talavera—confessor to Isabella
Fray Tomás de Torquemada—Grand Inquisitor of Spain

Other Rulers and Heads of State
John II, King of Portugal
Prince Henry the Navigator—leader of Portuguese exploration to the Indies
Henry II, King of France
Henry VII, King of England
Pope Alexander VI—the Borgia pope who mediated in the Treaty of Tordesillas

Geographers, Cosmographers and Mathematicians
Plato—Athenian philosopher, pupil of Socrates, teacher of Aristotle
Aristotle—Greek philosopher and scientist, author of *Treatise of Heaven and Earth*
Eratosthenes—Greek astronomer
Pythagoras—Greek philosopher and mathematician
Ptolemy—Alexandrine mathematician, astronomer, geographer, author of *Geographike Hyohegesis*
Al-Farghani—ninth century Arab scientist
Cardinal Pierre d'Ailly—author of *Imago Mundi*
Pavlo dal Pozzo Toscanelli—Florentine scientist
Jaime Ferrer—Catalan cosmographer
Abraham Zacuto—author of *Ephemerides* (astronomical almanac)
Dom Diogo Ortiz—Bishop of Ceuta and scientist to the King of Portugal
Master Rodrigo—astronomer and physician to the King of Portugal
José Vicinho—cosmographer and astronomer to the King of Portugal

The First Voyage
In the *Santa Maria*—Basque-built *nao* (nicknamed *La Gallega*—the Galician)
  Christopher Columbus—Admiral
  Juan de la Cosa—a Basque, owner and Master
  Peralonso Niño—of Moguer, Pilot
  Diego Chachu—Boatswain
  Juan Sánchez—of Cordova, Surgeon

Pedro de Terreros—Steward
Rodrigo Escobedo—Secretary and Royal representative*
Rodrigo de Sánchez—of Segovia, Royal representative
Pedro Gutiérrez—Royal representative*
Diego de Harana—of Cordova, Provost Marshal (cousin of Columbus's mistress)*
Luis de Torres—Interpreter (*converso*)

*Left at the settlement of Navidad with 36 men

In the *Santa Clara*—caravel (nicknamed *Nina*)
Vicente Yáñez Pinzón—of Palos, Captain
Juan Niño—of Moguer, owner and Master
Sancho Ruis de Gama—Pilot
Master Alonso—of Moguer, Surgeon

In the *Pinta*—caravel (known only by nickname)
Martin Alonso Pinzón—of Palos, Captain
Francisco Martin Pinzón—Master
Cristóbal Garcia Xalmiento—Pilot
Cristóbal Quintero—of Palos, owner and seaman
Juan Quintero—of Palos, Boatswain
Master Diego—Surgeon
Garcia Fernández—of Palos, Steward
Gómez Rascón—doubting seaman
Juan Pérez Viscaino—repaired the *Pinta* in the Canaries
Rodrigo de Triana—first man to sight land

In one of the three ships, not known which
Bartolomé de Torres—ex-convict
Bartholomé Roldán—ex-convict
Rodrigo de Jérez—of Ayamonte
Pedro de Villa
Ruy Garcia—of Santona
Jácome—executed at Navidad

The Second Voyage
Christopher Columbus
Diego Colón—younger brother of Columbus
Fray Bernado Buil—fleet chaplain
Dr Diego Alvarez Chanca—Royal Physician
Alonso de Ojeda—future conquistador
Juan de la Cosa—future cosmographer (*not* the owner of the *Santa Maria*)

Michele de Cuneo—friend of Columbus
Bernal de Pisa—Royal Inspector
Antonio de Torres—Commander of relief fleet
Fernando Pérez de Luna—Secretary and Public Notary
Don Bartolomeo Colón—brother of Columbus, with the relief fleet
Fray Ramón Pané
Juan Aguado—Royal representative
Alonso Sánchez de Carvajal—Shipmaster
The father and uncle of Bartholomé Las Casas

The Third Voyage
Christopher Columbus
Pedro de Terreros—Captain of the *Vaqueños* (70 tons), Steward of the *Santa Maria* on the first voyage
Hernan Péres—Captain of *El Correo*
Alonso Sánchez de Carvajal—ship captain (also served on second voyage)
Pedro de Harana—ship captain, brother of Columbus's mistress
Giovanni Antonio Colombo—Genoese ship captain
Amerigo Vespucci—fitted out this fleet but did not sail in it
Alonso Pérez—of Huelva, servant to Columbus
Don Bartolomeo Colón—Vice-Governor of Española, brother of Columbus
Francisco Roldán—Chief Justice in Española
Alonso de Ojeda—also on the second voyage
Francisco de Bobadilla—replacement as Governor for Columbus
Andres Martin—captain of ship that took Columbus back to Spain in disgrace
The father of Bartholomé Las Casas

The Fourth Voyage
Don Nicolas de Ovando—replacement Governor for Española

In *La Capitana*—caravel, flagship, 70 tons
    Christopher Columbus
    Diego Tristán—Captain (killed by natives at Belén)
    Ambrosyo Sánchez—Master
    Juan Sánchez—Chief Pilot
    Antón Donato—Quartermaster
    Master Bernal—Surgeon
    Don Fernando Colón—Columbus's natural son (aged 13)

In the *Santiago de Palos*—caravel, 60 tons (nicknamed *Bermuda*)
    Francisco de Porras—Captain

Diego de Porras—Fleet Accountant
Francisco Bermúdas—Master
Pedro Gómes—Quartermaster
Don Bartolomeo Colón—brother of Columbus
Diego Méndez—gentleman

In *La Gallega*—caravel, 60 tons (abandoned in River Belén)
Pedro de Terreros—Captain (also on first and third voyages)
Juan Quintero—Master (on the *Pinta* on the first voyage)
Alonso Ramón—Quartermaster

In the *Viscaýno*—caravel, 50 tons (abandoned at Puerto Bello)
Bartolomeo Fieschi—Genoese Captain, childhood friend of Columbus
Juan Pérez—Master
Martin de Fuenterabia—Quartermaster
Pedro de Ledesma—Pilot
Fray Alixandre—Priest

In Homebound Fleet
Antonio de Torres
Francisco de Bobadilla—ex-Governor
Francisco Roldán—rebel (also on the third voyage)
Sanchez de Carvajal

Native Chiefs on the Caribbean Islands
Guacanagari
Caonabó
Mayreni
Guarionex
Nacaona—female overlord
Ameyro—ruler of Jamaica

Other Explorers of the Period
Marco Polo—travelled to the land of the Great Khan, author of *Livre de Merveilles du Mond*
Bartholomeu Dias—Portuguese, first to round the Cape of Good Hope
Jean de Bethencourt—Norman knight, made conquests in the Canaries
Alonso de Lugo—conqueror in the Canaries
Hernan Peraza—Governor of Gomera
Vasco da Gama—Portuguese, first to reach India via the Cape of Good Hope
Vicente Yáñez Pinzón—discoverer of Brazil (also sailed on the first voyage)

Pedro Alvares Cabral—Portuguese, rival discoverer of Brazil
Peralonso Niño—made voyage to South America (also on the first voyage)
Alonso de Ojeda—made voyage to South America
Amerigo Vespucci—sailed with Ojeda to South America
Giovanni Caboto—Italian navigator, discovered North America with the
   backing of the City of Bristol

Index